THE CHURCH TAKES ROOT IN INDIA

THE CHURCH TAKES ROOT IN INDIA

BASIL JOSEPH MATHEWS

GYAN

Published by

GYAN

Gyan Publishing House
5, Ansari Road
Daryaganj, New Delhi-110002
Phone: 011-47034999, 9811692060
E-mail: books@gyanbooks.com

Distribution Network
gyanbooks.com
India, USA, Canada, UK, Australia

ISBN: 978-93-7014-691-4 (PB)

First Published, 1938

2nd Impression 2025

Printed at: Gyan Press, Delhi.

THE CHURCH TAKES ROOT IN INDIA
Author: BASIL JOSEPH MATHEWS

THE CHURCH TAKES ROOT IN INDIA

The Church Takes Root in India

Preface

THE VISITOR WHO HAS LOVED AND STUDIED INDIA FOR DECADES and then comes to it from the Western world sees the marvel of its uniqueness, the qualities that make its people and their life unlike any other. Yet, paradoxically, every contemporary force that we find in action in the West and the Far East, as well as in Africa, is also throwing new threads across the time-worn and lovely tapestry of the Indian past. Already a new pattern begins to emerge. As I moved to and fro across the wide spaces of that vast country and watched its peoples in the fields and villages, in the cities and on the roads, I knew that India would never let me go. Mr. Edward Thompson was greeted one day by Mr. Gandhi, who said, "I understand that you have published a book called *Farewell to India*." Mr. Thompson assented and Mr. Gandhi exclaimed, "You know that that is untrue. Never so long as you live will you be able to say good-by to India."

As the guest of Indian states and British administrators, of Congress leaders and ex-prisoners, of Communists, Christian missionaries, and village pastors, as a friend of leaders of Indian art and culture, as a visitor to schools and colleges, as a fellow-craftsman working at a task with editors and reporters, and in the company of pioneers of women's movements—Mohammedan, Hindu, Parsi, Christian—

Preface

I had the privilege of looking out on the landscape of India through windows opening from every angle.

It is tragic that multitudes of Western people live in India for many years yet spend their whole life there on a little island of exclusively white companionship. They never meet Indians face to face save as servants or shopkeepers. I feel it necessary to state my conviction that a few months in India, following a quarter of a century of study of her life, can give an infinitely truer and deeper knowledge of the country and its people than these exclusive Westerners achieve through a lifetime of residence. An English merchant's wife who has lived for decades in India reiterated to me day after day on the ship sailing to India, "Every Indian is in the last resort at heart a snake." She then, with an unconscious inconsistency at once sublime and ridiculous, told me of her own Indian personal servant who had saved her life in an earthquake at the imminent peril of his own. I carefully analyzed her statement, which is so convincing to the ordinary traveler: "I have lived for years among Indians, so I *know*." The real truth is that she sees Indians through a triplex glass compounded of race-pride, middle-class caste arrogance, and ignorant muddle-headedness.

This little book does not attempt to record those impressions of personalities and trends which I have already done elsewhere[1] in collaboration with Miss Winifred Wilson, who brought another angle of vision to the survey of the

[1] In *India Reveals Herself*, New York, Oxford University Press, 1937.

scene. I am grateful to editors and secretaries connected with the foreign mission boards of North America for material that brings our knowledge of contemporary movements in India up to date of publication.

What is here essayed is a picture of that swiftly growing Christian community in India whose influence is already out of all proportion to its numbers and whose membership increases with such startling speed. In particular I have tried to present an intimate first-hand understanding of the complex of human relations that give inexhaustible fascination to the Indian village, which will be the inevitable foundation of the new India as it has been of the old.

Even after exercising all possible care to be accurate and scrupulously fair I would have hesitated to send this book out had not the Bishop of Dornakal (Dr. Azariah), the Reverend J. Z. Hodge (Secretary of the National Christian Council of India, Burma and Ceylon), the Reverend William Paton, Dr. Nicol Macnicol, and the Reverend C. W. Posnett, with prodigal generosity given many hours of their time to reading the manuscript at successive stages. In the case of the first two named, I had the benefit of going over the first draft of the manuscript with them personally. To all these and to the uncounted friends in India whose guidance and companionship I have enjoyed and hope to continue to share, I owe deep gratitude.

Basil Mathews

Boston
March, 1938

CONTENTS

PRELUDE

This book is a study of a newly emerging India; and, for that reason, it is affected throughout by the world turmoil in which we are all engulfed. For in India today, whether you plunge into politics, engage in business, or work and play as a student in school or college; whether you listen to the talk of the peasant-farmers at the end of the day's work, or join in the songs and prayers of the village Christian community, you are caught in the mesh of the world's life. A new absorbing drama of opposing wills and purposes is carrying India through passionate and at times tragic scenes to a still unguessed climax. That drama reveals the impact of destructive forces and creative ideas from the West upon the ancient ways of life of India. The immemorial life flows on—but not unchanged. The new India that will one day emerge will in turn help to reshape the world that is now destroying her ancient rhythm.

India may become the central arena of the contemporary world struggle for the supremacy of the spiritual and of the moral in the life of man. That struggle is at a crisis in the Far East and in the West. India with her ancient wisdom and her spirited vision stands between these troubled peoples. It would, indeed, seem natural that the spiritual destinies of Asia may be largely determined by that great Indian people, now a sixth of the human race.

India is no longer patient and receptive; she is explosive and expressive. Over two thousand years ago her creative and missionary energy gave to Burma, Ceylon, and China, and through China to Japan, the religion of Buddha that has been the dominant spiritual faith of the Far East ever since. What will India give today toward the glorious task of shaping the new world?

Words from one of the letters of the great Indian nationalist and socialist, Pundit Jawaharlal Nehru, to his daughter Indira, now an undergraduate in Oxford University, restate this question in face of the emerging India of tomorrow:

There is no peace for us in this turbulent twentieth century, a third of which has already passed with its full complement of war and revolution. "The whole world is in revolution," says the great Fascist, Mussolini; "events themselves are a tremendous force pushing us on like some implacable will." And the great Communist, Trotsky, also warns us of this century not to expect too much of peace and comfort. "It is clear," he says, "that the twentieth century is the most disturbed century within the memory of humanity. Any contemporary of ours who wants peace and comfort before everything else has chosen a bad time to be born."

The whole world is in labor and the shadow of war and revolution lies heavy everywhere. If we cannot escape from this unenviable destiny of ours, how shall we face it? Ostrich-like, shall we hide our heads from it? Or shall we play a brave part in the shaping of events and, facing risks and perils if need be, have the joy of great and noble adventure, and the feeling that our "steps are merging with those of history"?[1]

A glimpse of the future place of the Christian church in India in this shaping of world events was symbolized in the University Church at Oxford in the summer of 1937 at the World Conference on Church, Community and State. At the celebration of the Holy Communion by the Archbishop of Canterbury we took the bread and the wine at the hand of the Bishop of Dornakal in fellowship with Negro and French, Chinese and Japanese, Scandinavian, American and British, Russian and Korean. As we of so many races and nations received the emblem of the eternal sacrifice and of everlasting life at the hands of this Indian fellow-Christian, we knew ourselves to be members of a world community—the universal church.

That world comradeship is not international or interracial in the sense of an organization that, from without, federates diverse elements. It is a living organism. The church of the disciples of Christ is one, as the body is one, by virtue of the one life that flows through all the limbs. We have no word for this world oneness that is created from the heart, save the clumsy word "ecumenical."

When ancient Greece and Hellenized Rome used the word ecumene, they were trying to express the oneness of

[1] *Glimpses of World History*. Allahabad, 1935.

a civilization that lived by virtue of a luminous central standard of values. That radiant source shaped and gave meaning to the life of the individual and of the community. So when we use the word "ecumenical" we are trying to express the sacred mystery of the oneness of the church in Christ. And the rapidly growing church in India is leading the universal church toward realized oneness.

As we at Oxford, however, contemplated the world into which those men and women would return from that service, we knew that tragic separation defies such oneness. The Negro would go back home to find again that he was barred in parts of his native land, whether Africa or America, from access to Holy Communion in company with white Christians. The Indian would go back to find—in spite of much miraculous unity—in some churches caste separation as between Indians, and in some other churches, race separatism. The Japanese and the Chinese would go back to find the divine State in a mystical totalitarian form claiming absolute authority over all the life of all its subjects and so denying that sovereignty of Christ which is the root of our unity.

Here is the focal point of the world opportunity of each of us as members of that church. Our generation is the first in the nineteen hundred years of Christian history to see the church in actual living reality rooted in every habitable part of the globe. The universal church exists at last. The Indian church is in the center of it. It has come into being, not through armchair discussion, but through the sustained heroic lives of thousands of missionaries in all continents. The Indian church is now itself a strongly missionary body. Yet the universal church is divided within; and it is threatened from without by implacable foes in Europe and the Americas as well as in Asia and Africa. But it is increasingly clear that in the forces that the church can release lies mankind's one hope.

To live for the church's oneness and for her integrity is, therefore, central. She is moving today, to a degree not yet fully realized, toward a common mind and purpose. Under the blows and threats of a universal paganism, we see more clearly that we who were "aliens and foreigners" are "members of the household of God." In this book we shall try to see the increasing part to be played by that church in India and by those from the West who go out to serve her and to strengthen her arm. She is increasingly realizing her own spiritual genius and preparing to share the fruits of that spirit with all mankind.

Chapter One

THE RHYTHM OF VILLAGE LIFE

As the western visitor walks toward an Indian village, he sees the men harvesting in the fields and the women gleaning behind them. He gazes at the golden dust that the homeward-going cattle raise in the afternoon sunlight, hears the splash of water from the goatskin bags used for irrigating the gardens, and the thud that announces that the washerman is hammering clothes on the flat stone at the river's edge. The rhythm of Indian peasant life begins to beat in his consciousness. Not until one has spent a life service in India, however, does one begin to realize the sensitive, closely woven mesh of interrelated responsibilities, rights, and duties that have for at least two thousand years been the resistant fabric of India's life.

I

In every land the peasant is moving to a new outlook. Revolutionary leaders know that success depends upon swinging the peasant's will to the support of change.

Before we can assess the significance of the forces that are changing India we need to understand the values as well as the weaknesses of the ancient village life. We now examine a village living that life unchanged. We shall then, in the next chapter, watch new leavens at their transforming work.

We see the children running in and out of little village houses that may be only a year or two old, yet are the most ancient of all the homes of the Indian. They are small mud huts, each some ten feet by twelve or more, with a mud veranda shaded by the extension of the palm or thatch roof beyond the low house-wall. The monsoons of a thousand successive seasons may wash millions of these huts away; but always the new home goes up on the persistent pattern; and what was, is, and will be.

The woman of the house smears the floor of the hut with a blend of mud, water, and cow-dung. She is proud of her jars and bowls of dull red or polished black earthenware that stand on the floor. Some brass trays and copper cooking-pots, industriously rubbed to a high sheen, adorn the less poverty-stricken homes. In one corner is the place where the family stand to bathe, pouring water over the head and trunk. In another corner is the tiny mud cooking place, of horseshoe shape—unless, as often is the case, the cooking is done outside. After his day's ploughing the husband is resting in a corner of the veranda on a *charpoy*, the Indian bed or settee made of a rough wooden oblong frame set on four short sturdy legs, with tough cord interlaced across the width and down the length of the oblong.

A hut like that is home for well-nigh three hundred

million people[1] in the seven hundred thousand villages of India. A great part of the time of the family, of course, is spent not in the home but in the open air, on the veranda or working on the land.

Outside the village proper are the rude broken-down shelters of the outcastes, where the most meager necessity of life (a flimsy cover from the sun or the rain) is all that can be achieved.

One or more elaborate homes grace most villages, belonging to more prosperous family groups—the Indian larger family unit of as many as eighty people, comprising all the descendants from one living ancestor. These houses are built in the shape of a small quadrangle. They shelter the family from the outside world by largely windowless walls. The inner court, where there is sometimes a well, is surrounded by a veranda. Behind this center of infinite gossip are the private living rooms of the great-grandparents, grandparents, any unmarried daughters, and the families of the married sons. The chapel or worship room, the storerooms, and the kitchens are also here. If the family still grows and bursts the bounds of this court, the wall may be broken through and a passage made, beyond which is built a further quadrangle similarly surrounded by rooms. Into these courts the goats and oxen may be brought at night for security.

Here, then, is a village of, let us say, one hundred and

[1] The total population of India, including Burma, is about three hundred and fifty-two millions. See statistical tables at end of book.

sixty families.[1] They are divided into perhaps twelve or more castes. If the representatives of a single one of those castes leave the village or die out, it becomes vital for that community either to plead with a man of that caste from another village to come over at intervals to work there, or actually to import him and his family. For each caste has its work to do. No other caste must do that work, and the work of each caste is essential. The sum-total of their industry suffices for all the demands—spiritual, social, and physical—of the Hindu village community. Thus we see that the caste system is the solid basis of Hindu society. It ordains all the details of a man's life; it fixes and regulates his occupation; it prescribes his gods and his religious duties. To the Brahmans, the outcastes, of which there are fifty-two millions in India, are barely human and have no part in the divine order of Hindu society. To touch an outcaste is pollution to a caste Hindu. The outcaste group in a village have strictly segregated quarters, and may not approach either the temples, the wells, or the tanks of the caste people.

The Hindu village community is a pattern based on the principle of graded interdependence, similar in ideal to St. Paul's picture of the graded mutual service of the limbs in a body. "The eye cannot say to the hand, I have no

[1] The description that follows is precisely true of multitudes of villages. It would require modification to be strictly accurate for multitudes of other villages. The system, however, with its clearly defined occupational responsibilities and hereditary rights, known as the *jajmani* system, is fundamentally the same everywhere.

need of thee: or again the head to the feet, I have no need of you."[1] But in the Pauline picture there are no outcastes.

We have come into the village at an interesting time for helping us to grasp how this unique system works. For along the path to the granary of one of the Brahman peasant-farmers winds a little stream of men, as happens at seasonal intervals. First, comes a carpenter. His fathers for centuries have made and mended the ploughs of the ancestors of this farmer. The farmer weighs out to him ten and a half pounds of grain for every plough that the carpenter has kept in repair through the season of cultivation. Behind him again comes the barber, who has shaved the farmer's face twice a week through the year, and cut his hair once a month. The barber is also a match-making intermediary between families. His wife, too, has served the farmer's family, for she has oiled the body of the Brahman's wife and shampooed her hair; while if any baby has come in the family she has massaged both the baby and the mother for weeks after the birth. So the farmer weighs out to him seven pounds of barley, fourteen pounds of wheat, and seven pounds of rice. More and more frequently today payment in money is made in the Indian village. This growing practice is not fully prevalent, but in proportion to its growth it weakens the system that we are describing.

The bent form of a potter now approaches. All through the year he has carried up from the river bed on the back of his donkey the muddy clay which he has shaped on

[1] *I Corinthians* 12:21.

his potter's wheel into the round fat water jars, the shallow saucer-lamps, the cooking casseroles used by the womenfolk, and even the bowl of the Brahman's pipe. The payment in kind to the potter is about equal to that of the barber. Standing at a distance humbly is the low-caste *dhobi*, the washerman. Throughout the year he has collected the dirty clothes from the farmer's home, carried them on the back of his starved-looking donkey, soaked them overnight, beaten them upon his dhobi-board, or a flat stone by the river's edge, and spread them out on the ground in the sun to dry. His labor is incessant, and from the farmer he gets in grain the equivalent to the carpenter's reward for mending the plough, that is, some ten and a half pounds of grain.

If we are ignorant of Indian village life we are astonished to see the florist come for his reward. What place has a florist in the Indian village? Perhaps the Western visitor will now self-consciously put his hand to his neck, where hangs the garland of flowers with which he has been decked with ceremonial hospitality on entering the village. The florist grew them. At every wedding the bridegroom's floral headdress and the flowers of all the villagers come from the florist's garden. Whenever the Brahman priest invests a growing boy with the sacred thread of manhood over his left shoulder the florist must bring his mango flowers and leaves. From his garden also come the *mendhi* leaves from which is derived the henna that reddens the toe-nails and finger-nails of the bride and groom, and is rubbed on the scalp of the bride where the hair is parted to show that she is now married. Indeed, there are few women in the village who do not go quietly to the florist or send to him for henna, which they use as a cosmetic.

Two proud specialists now approach: the vegetable-grower and the rice-grower. Well-to-do farmers will hire some portion of the time of these men to improve their own crops. We are startled to find that there is one caste wholly given up to the occupation of grain-parching. What are called in the West puffed rice and popcorn are extremely popular with the vegetarian Hindu, and most villages have their grain-parching specialist.

The next man who comes to the farmer for his reward is more accurately called a sewing-man than a tailor. The reason for this is, of course, that a major part of the raiment of Indian people, whether men or women, is composed of long straight pieces of cotton or silk fabric, simply hemmed round the edges. However, shirts of various designs need to be made for men and boys, and jackets for the women and girls; though no great flexibility of mind is needed to catch up with new fashions—for there are none.

Our little procession of village citizens has not yet passed. Here come two or three others. The village has need of only one oil-presser, but he is essential. Without the oil that he presses from the seeds of the mustard, the sesamum, and the castor plants, what would the barber's wife do for her massage, the housewife for her saucer lamp, the water-carrier for softening the leather bags, and the farmer for oiling the wheels of his bullock cart?

Among the poorest of the poor are the water-carriers, in whose families the women bear the water to the homes of the better-off inhabitants and the men help to irrigate the fields. Lower than any of these we have named are two utterly outcaste groups—the leather-workers and the scavengers. The leather-workers skin dead animals, sell and mend leather bags, spread manure in the fields, make sun-baked bricks, feed cattle and are, so to speak, at the beck and call of their lords, the Brahmans and even the middle-caste peasants. They are the field slaves of the village. Below even these are the scavengers, whose daily task it is to clean the cesspools of the village and to drive the swine every morning scavenging through the village to clean up the filth deposited during the night. In numerous villages these lowest of the low are beginning to find a new economic freedom by going to neighboring towns as servants to Europeans. In such cases their absence serves to reveal to the village community how essential they are to its health; for no other group, whether caste or outcaste, is allowed by Hinduism to pollute itself by carrying out their work.

Meanwhile we have not looked at all at the function either of those few castes whose service is paid for at the time that it is rendered or of the Brahman farmer himself. In this village is a goldsmith who makes the gold *tali*, the symbol equivalent to the wedding ring, which is placed around the neck of the bride. He also hammers bangles out of gold or silver for the children and womenfolk, makes metal filigree, and sets precious stones. To the village woman he has always been an important man, for to the Indian woman her jewelry is not merely ornament. If divorced she can carry away with her all that is on her person. Wearing her bangles and bracelets she is, so to speak, her own traveling bank.

Aloof from all these people is a high-caste man—the village accountant, who keeps the village land records and is responsible to the government district officer for the assessment of taxes. It is at this point that we recognize one of the changes which an alien government has brought into the old, coherent, static system. For the accountant is not a part of this interdependent socio-economic pattern; he neither renders to the village services without which it could not function, nor does he depend on it for his support.

As we look at the Brahman who has been the focus of our procession, we discover a similar change. The Brahman has the right and duty to sacrifice to the gods for the villages and to teach them the sacred law. The right to sacrifice he still exercises. No wedding or funeral or festival can take place without his services coming into play; while he alone can invest with the sacred thread the sons of the "twice-born." In villages even where there is no temple he is thus the family priest. His other function of teaching, however, is being thrust persistently into the background. The learning of the secular government teacher, however meager, puts at a discount the repetition of the traditional holy books by the Brahman.

The functions of the Brahman and the fees that he receives for his duties as family priest are relatively so small as to make it impossible nowadays for most Brahmans to live by their spiritual labors. Out of, say, forty Brahman families in a typical village, only some three or four of the men may be required to serve the total of perhaps one hundred and forty families. For this reason the vast majority of the village Brahmans of India are farmers and cattle-feeders. In addition they often become money-lenders. The peasant requires solid cash to pay his taxes, to buy seed and bullocks, to meet the often fantastically extravagant costs of family weddings and dowries, to pay the goldsmith for bangles for his womenfolk. So he goes to the Brahman farmer and secures a loan. Unfortunately, he usually has to pay a rate of interest that strains his resources to the limit, to say nothing of repaying the original sum borrowed. Thus the peasant lapses into economic servitude that all too often descends from him to his children. This means that when he goes at harvest time to receive from the Brahman the grain due to him for his services during the year, he may receive often barely enough to keep body and soul together, in place of the heap that he has earned. As money-lender the Brahman takes out part of his interest in kind. Rabindranath Tagore is reported to have said, "The Brahmans have forgotten their responsibilities but they remember their demands. The cow ceases to give milk, but we feel the pressure of her horn."

II

When we examine the intricate pattern of rights and responsibilities in this village, gradually there shines through it the clue to its persistence across the centuries. Every tiny family group has a hereditary clientèle whom it serves as did its ancestors, and from whom it takes sustenance. In some cases there is not even payment by grain for service, but service is rendered for service. The barber shaves the washerman, who washes the barber's clothes. He shaves the grain-parcher, who in return "pops" his corn and "puffs" his rice. He shaves the potter, and in return finds a water-pot upon his threshold.

In practice almost everybody serves and has the right to be served by almost everyone else, except that the lowest castes and the outcastes have little done for them. If, for instance, we follow the carpenter through his year of work, we find that he has helped the farmer by making handles for his sickles and hoes, and yokes for his oxen. He has also made door frames and doors, wall pegs and water spouts for the village houses. The *chapaties*[1] have been rolled upon a board that he has made and with a rolling pin that he has supplied. The villagers sleep on

[1] The thin round cakes that are the bread of India.

beds whose frames he has put together, and the peasant and his grain go to market in bullock carts whose bodies and wheels he has shaped.

The attachment of each peasant to his own particular village is intensified by an alluring group of rights—concessions which are made to him freely by the community. He has, for instance, a free site for his little house, freedom to gather fruit from some sixteen different kinds of uncultivated fruit trees like the mango, free grazing with fodder rights, and the carpenter often has access to timber. By this wonderful integration the community has in its hand a weapon for controlling its unruly members. This weapon when used in 1925 and 1931 through the genius of Mr. Gandhi even brought the British government up short. It is the power of boycott. No member of the village, as we have seen, can live at all without the services of others. The moment the community decides to ostracize him, he can only survive by flight or submission. And flight merely leads him to an uneasy effort to penetrate another closed group, unless he goes into organized industry where caste distinctions are blurred.

This throws light on the almost intolerable situation of a man in a Hindu village who decides to become a Christian. In doing so he is caught in the remorseless pressure of this Hindu economic and social boycott unless, as we shall see later, he comes to the Christian church in the company of his social group, in what is by a misnomer called a mass movement. When that happens the group carry their social pattern of mutual service with them. In the past, the ostracism of an isolated convert has forced the missionary organization to assume responsibility for him and his family by taking him into service. A calamitous result has been that these Christian converts have naturally tended to live apart from the main stream of Indian life. But what other course could they have taken when cast out by the Hindu or Moslem community?

One evil that shackles the peasant's feet and ties one hand, so to speak, behind his back, is the fearful effect of the doctrine of *ahimsa*, or non-injury of any living thing. The root of *ahimsa* is the idea of the unity and therefore the ultimate sacredness of all being.

As a result some two hundred million underdeveloped and largely unproductive cattle must not be slain because they are sacred. Numberless hordes of monkeys raid orchards. Billions of rats consume at least ten per cent of the grain harvest and spread the dreaded plague. Flocks of crows and herds of wild deer and wild hogs raid the defenseless peasant's crops, and hold from school the boys who have to spend their days driving the marauding creatures from their fathers' fields. Even on economic grounds village India needs to substitute for the false doctrine that gives all sentient life equal value, the realistic doctrine of the book of *Genesis* that man shall have "dominion over every living thing that moveth upon the earth."

The characteristic court of village India is the *panchayat*, or literally, group of five. This village council has existed time out of mind for settling internal disputes, for supervising communal activities such as the repair of the irrigation tanks of the village, as well as for representing the villagers in their dealings with the tax-collectors.

The coming of British rule, with its law courts and Indian lawyers educated in Western ways, made this ancient customary *panchayat* crumble away. Something resembling anarchy arose. At last the government, after rather clumsy and top-heavy experiments, launched during the World War experimental *panchayats* that now have become the standard unit of village self-government throughout India. In some places the unit is one village, and in others a group of villages; their powers vary slightly according to the different provinces, normally including administrative and judicial authority.

When, for example, a quarrel arises between two villagers, the accuser and the defendant each choose two men, while the village headman makes the fifth and presides at the inquiry. Each man states his case and is questioned. Then the *panchayat* discusses it.

Its members, who have lived in the village all their lives, know who are the rogues, the "slackers," the most unscrupulous liars in the village. By and large (even if at times the arch-rogue of the village may be himself in the *panchayat*) they are able to "spot" the real offender, and are likely to see the best middle way toward a solution of some village imbroglio. No verdict is valid that is not unanimous. It often takes the form of a compromise between the parties. The British legal system in India gives absolute support to the decision of the *panchayat*, which no high court judge ever dreams of reversing.

One thing that is weakening the *panchayat's* position in the village is the tendency of the plaintiff who has a weak case to run off to the professional "pleader," who will bring the case before a court in which it is often easier to introduce bribed witnesses—a court where the local circumstances are unknown.

As we watch the village organism thus functioning almost like the members of the human body, admiration for its many humane qualities deepens. What our modern poor law, health insurance and unemployment relief do clumsily for the colossus of the Western nation, this Hindu *jajmani* system does automatically in the manageable dimensions of each tiny group of the seven hundred thousand villages of India. A growing boy or girl feels himself or herself to be not so much an individual person as a corpuscle in the blood-stream of the family-clan. Every step of his or her life from birth to marriage is controlled by the family under the authority of its head. Yet whereas our standard of values includes the right and duty of the individual by his own initiative to achieve self-expression for the service of the world, we discover that the Indian village automatically stifles any such adventure.

One aspect of this is shown in the experience of Dr. W. H. Wiser, whose book, *The Hindu Jajmani System*, presents the most penetrating analysis yet achieved of the pattern of life in an Indian village.[1] His power to reveal the detailed working of the system was of priceless value as I watched the peasants moving to and fro performing their functions in the life of the village.

Some caste villagers refused to allow their children to attend a school where a Christian outcaste boy (a Bhangi, or scavenger) had a place. "It is against the will of God," they said, "that untouchables should read." And then, in sentences that reveal the Hindu religious background of the whole system, exclaimed, "Why, if Bhangis are to read, have we all been created different? Why did God create carpenters, grain-parchers, potters, barbers, cattle-men and the like? Did God not intend that each should perform his own work? Certainly it is not necessary for a Bhangi to read when his work is to clean cesspools."

We see from this speech of the peasants that Hinduism is made up not alone of the ideas and laws of thousands of years ago gathered in the sacred books of Hinduism that define and support this system, but includes this social and economic system itself. Hinduism is, indeed, the total fabric of spiritual law, immemorial custom, and contemporary habit. The maintenance of peaceful order was the goal of the creative thinkers whose philosophy we find in those sacred books. The divisions between high caste, middle

[1] Dr. and Mrs. Wiser's unsurpassed intimacy with village life, combined with their scientific economic mastery, give this book a unique place. Without its illumination I could not have given a coherent picture of the complicated relationships comprised in the *jajmani* system.

and low caste, as well as the suppression of the outcaste, probably have prehistoric roots in a blend of the desires to maintain racial purity and sustain the integrity of faith and culture. *Varna*, the Sanskrit for caste, means color.

The castes are today, as we have seen, hereditary occupational groups. If a man is a goldsmith or a vegetable-grower, probably his earliest ancestor was one. It might in one sense be said that the very core of Hinduism is to do your duty in the caste to which God has called you. The highest duty of a Sudra (a man from the lowest of the four great castes) is to serve Brahmans. If he does this he will, according to the Hindu teaching of the transmigration of souls, be reborn in a higher caste.

III

When we set ourselves the fascinating task of assessing the values of this system, we are baffled because we are in the cross-current of two contradictions. Here are human relationships woven into a coherent system of mutual service. Strictly speaking this cannot be called cooperation: for it is the separate performance of one's own inherited function, in which no one else can share, but without which village life, based on caste, cannot persist.

Reinforced by the doctrine of *karma*,[1] with its sense of

[1] The doctrine that all actions bear inevitable fruit. Everything experienced in each successive life is rigidly determined by the acts of a past life and forms the expiation of them. Sin is punished by an utterly immovable law.

the inevitability of whatever is one's fate, the system results in a considerable measure of contentment. As contrasted with the insecurity prevailing in the West it produces an enviable security which, while it leaves little room for individual initiative, protects and upholds the individual in carrying out some functions of his manhood. It has to be confessed, however, that in practice the reciprocity is limited. If famine threatens the group, the outcaste has to take the brunt. The fatherly feeling of the lord for his serf that generally prevailed in medieval England, for example, is not so visible in the caste system. But in ordinary times the fact that a gesture of, for instance, pouring water from the caste well into the outcaste's water-jar is believed to bring merit to the caste man who performs it, does to some degree mitigate the harshness of the exclusion of the outcaste from the ranks of Hindu humanity.

The nostalgia of millions of cultivated Europeans and Americans for the static civilization of the Middle Ages, with its creative handicrafts and ordered relationships, is a longing for the things that twentieth-century Hindu civilization still possesses.

Like a persistent haunting theme in a symphony is the quest of beauty by the Indian peasant and craftsman. We feel an anguish of pity for the undernourished Indian villager perpetually fending from his hearth the insistent wolf of hunger. We are exasperated at his rejection of improved ways of growing crops and breeding beasts that would double his food supply. But then suddenly he lifts our spirit by his pursuit of the beautiful. That quest sings in his religious lyrics and in the language of the stories of his gods. Grace, which is beauty in motion, swings in the folds of a woman's *sari,* shines in its coloring, and curves in the restrained gesture of a dance. Beauty is revealed in the contour of a water-pot and the line of the thatch on a roof. It is woven into the texture of a basket; and is patiently hammered out in the pattern on a copper tray.

As we gaze into the heart of this coherent interdependent system how well we can understand the longing of a Gandhi to hold back "satanic" mechanistic industrialism, which—as we shall now see—is threatening its destruction. Western man has taken five centuries to move from the Middle Ages to our mechanistic modernism. Unwittingly the West is forcing that transition upon India in terms not of centuries but of decades. Millions of young Indians, who were born and reared in childhood under this *jajmani* system which we have just described, live today in an ever changing world being remade by Marconi and Marx, Henry Ford and Metro-Goldwyn-Mayer. Individualism and self-assertion are seeping from the American and British Far West and the Japanese Far East into India. As we see demonic forces driving the West and the Far East toward world war, may we not pause to ask whether the central values of the static peaceful Indian order of life should not be protected?

Chapter Two

THE CHANGING TEMPO

I

OUTSIDE THE CITY GATE OF OLD DELHI, THE SPACE WHERE the camel caravans used to halt is now full of motor buses. They weave their way to and from practically every village within a radius of one hundred miles. Every day multitudes of village people climb into this triumph of scientific mechanism, the product of an utterly different conception of life from that which keeps India loyal to the primitive wooden plough and the ways of life of a thousand years ago. Educators, village pastors, pioneer workers in rural reconstruction, and doctors from all parts of the land with whom I talked agreed in the judgment that the motor bus is the most potent single instrument for change that was not present in India twenty years ago.

The villagers are swept along in the bus to a city. They find shop windows full of the products of machines. Against these, in the bazaars, the hand-made products of the coppersmith, the leather-worker, and the weaver sustain a brave battle. In Lahore, for instance, that conflict comes home to anyone who will walk out of the modern boulevard, with its policemen striving to control the motor traffic, into the medieval canyons of the ancient city, where you must stand aside to let the Afghan and his camel pass. The tide flows steadily away from the caravansary and toward the garage.

There is a crossroad in Lahore where, if a youth turns to the left, he comes to the exquisite beauty of line and color of an ancient mosque. At the marble water-tank in the courtyard the Moslem faithful perform their ceremonial cleansing. If, however, instead of turning left, the young man turns to the right he will reach the dazzling plaster façade of the motion picture theatre where the latest films of Conrad Veidt, Robert Taylor, and Charles Laughton, Katharine Hepburn and Madeleine Carroll lure him into the polytheistic temple where movie fans adore their chosen "star."

A curious illustration of this new "worship" is given by the experience of a Brahman girl, who in 1938, at the age of eighteen, has been a movie star for seven years. So great is her reputation that she cannot go to school to learn English (with a view to Hollywood), because she would be mobbed by the crowd of her "fans." Her brother, who watches carefully over her, brought her to missionaries in order that they might help her out of this difficulty.

On the edge of Lahore, where Kipling's Kim climbed across the rooftops in his detective work, his present counterpart drifts in from a neighboring village to the movies. There the settled convictions of his fathers are overturned. In one crowded hour he passes from a Western gangster film to a passionate drama of love. The advertisement of an Indian film that lies before me in the current issue of *The Congress Socialist* declares: "You will need more than one heart to store the emotions which are let loose in this wonderful passion play of the season." The ruling Indian pattern of relations between the sexes, the attitude of youth to age, and the dominance of custom over initiative, all suffer sledgehammer blows. Yet the Western civilization that produces the films displays its own moral bankruptcy in the gangster and the "vamp." India itself stands today sixth in the world in the actual production of films. To a decreasing degree these are concerned with reproducing rather clumsily the ancient mythologies of Krishna, Shiva, and the other deities. Increasingly they concentrate on the comedy and tragedy of Indian life today.

The short newsreel sweeps the watching Indian youth from motor-racing on Daytona Beach to American-built airplanes being flown by young Chinese officers fighting Japanese aggression. From watching the achievement of Soviet fliers between Moscow and the North Pole he passes to the building of a titanic dam in the Mississippi Valley. There opens to him a new world, more amazing than all the mythologies, and longing stirs in him to share in its adventurous enterprises.

When traveling on a long train journey in the company of an agent for a British-American company selling crude oil, I learned still more of the penetration of the machine even into agriculture. He showed me, here an engine, run on crude oil, grinding grain, and there another threshing barley and rice. Farther on, I saw a third drawing water for irrigation. At a later date I found one running lathes in a village workshop. In all cases village-born Indians were running the engines.

These machines—buses, motion pictures, power engines —call for the service of mechanics, trained to scientific precision and to the exact use of high-speed tools. The railway system that carries to and fro on pilgrimage and on business over six hundred million Indian passengers every year employs thousands of mechanics. Not only are the youths who become mechanics changed in outlook, but the incessant travel of India's millions on buses and crowded trains tends to break down caste exclusiveness. Mechanical transport weaves a sense of identity as a nation across all the provincial and religious separatism, and the linguistic and racial divisions of India.

Life and death for the peasant-farmer have always hung on the fickle incidence of the monsoon rains. The local village, remote, unrelated to other distant areas where rain might have fallen, used to suffer the horrors of famine when the rains failed. Three recent changes make that impossible today. Under unified administration bringing peace and security, persons and goods can be moved from any part of India to any other part where they are needed. Transport by rail and lorry, as well as by coastal steamship, and the communication of need by telegram and telephone constitute the second factor. The third is irrigation. Few people, whether Indian or European, realize the majestic scope of the operations by which the government has made fifty-five million acres of desert land—equal to eleven times the cultivable area of all Egypt—bear crops to feed her ever increasing population. We are bound to welcome these new processes; yet inevitably by the introduction of money exchange, intercommunication, and machinery, they tend to break down the self-contained village system that we have described; for that system is based on the exchange of goods and services between men born in a fixed hereditary status.

I passed wonderingly, in Mysore State, through villages whose tiny booths for the sale of sweetmeats and grain were lighted by electricity, and where the tailor turned on a switch to start his electric sewing-machine. The sheer presence of such things in a village breaks down something of the ancient structure of habit and outlook. But how, I asked, could villagers in the heart of India, remote from any city, secure and pay for electric power and light? The secret was revealed when I came upon the great hydro-electric works that harness the waters of the Cauvery River in Mysore State and generate 66,000 h.p. of electrical energy. Mysore State has its traveling missionaries spreading the knowledge of electricity, and persuading the village people to avail themselves of its use at fantastically low cost, which nevertheless yields to the government adequate profits.

If we follow the cables that carry this power in Mysore to either the Kolar gold mines, the sugar factory, the soap and silk factories and those for the manufacture of cement, paper, and porcelain, we see one of the transforming influences of India today—modern industrialism drawing the primitive villager from his field and handicraft occupations to become a small part of the world's labor machine. From the greatest concentration of cotton mills in the world, at Bombay, to the jute mills of the Hooghly River and to the Tata iron and steel works in Bihar, India today is increasingly industrialized. No exact statistics are possible because of the vague frontier between industry and craftsmanship. Mines, plantations, and organized industrial establishments having a personnel of ten or more employ today some five million persons, which is an increase of about thirty per cent in ten years.

The majority, however, of those men and women whom I watched in Madras tending the whirring power looms, or whose crowded tenements I visited in Bombay, have their real roots in the village. Their influence to change the village is therefore greater than it would be if they had left it permanently. They return sooner or later to their village home with a profoundly altered habit of life. They have received wages instead of being paid for their services by the services of others.[1] They have deserted the skilled craftsmanship of plough or chisel for the maddening monotony of automatic repetition. They perform one tiny

[1] See Chapter One.

task in a mechanical process. The tenacious tentacles of the larger family group and the grip of local public opinion are shaken off. In the city, the individual gains some freedom from ancient custom. But he becomes a mere number in a catalogue of wage-earners. He has no more will than a cog in an impersonal machine. He is a sterile, isolated grain of sand, instead of a part of the productive common soil. The young man who has learned the scientific law of the industrial machine can never again really live happily in the ancient pattern of village custom.

The factory invades the life even of those who stay in their villages. In the year when Mr. Gandhi pleaded with the people of India to go back to the old simple saucer lamp, her villages imported from the West hundreds of thousands of hurricane lamps. Simultaneously, miles of Japanese cotton fabric in imitation of *khaddar*[1] drape the bodies of India's peasants. The farmers are using hoes that come in increasing numbers from the iron foundries of the West. These changes begin to strike at the root of the village life described in the first chapter. They aim indeed a double blow. The imported lamp, the fabric, and the hoe begin to put out of work the village potter, the weaver, and the ironsmith. The purchase of factory-made goods withdraws from the village economy just that amount of money which bridges the gulf between nourishment and anemia.

[1] Strictly speaking, cloth spun and woven by hand in India from cotton grown in India.

II

By a curious paradox the mechanisms of transport carry into the villages the ferment of those doctrines of soul-force and of anti-mechanistic simplicity which lie deep in Mr. Gandhi's belief and teaching. The printing-press is a mechanism used in the production of his weekly paper, *Harijan,* through which he pours out to the world a stream of comment on events and opinions. His message, proclaimed mainly through the press and therefore dependent on the machine for its wide influence, holds up the picture of a united self-governing India, purged of the evils of a machine age. This seeming incongruity is characteristic of the interaction of opposites that India experiences to-day. Western mechanism, burrowing from without, is breaking up the ancient forms of Hinduism. Mr. Gandhi is fighting for reforms to change the life of Hinduism from within by bringing over fifty million outcastes within her gates.

Again and again in his recent campaigns for the removal of untouchability and for the opening of the temples of Hinduism to the depressed classes, Mr. Gandhi has shown that genius for dramatization which is a mark of supreme leadership. For example, on one occasion he was to speak to a great multitude in a *pandal,* a huge temporary structure of bamboo, open on all four sides and covered by a mat roof. As he took his place he saw a group of poor peasants standing outside. He asked the organizer of the meeting to bring them in. The man, confused yet nevertheless firm, said that "even to obey an order from the Mahatma[1] himself," he dare not bring them in, for they were outcastes and their presence would empty the *pandal*. Instantly, Gandhi left the platform and went to stand among the outcastes; and from that position he delivered his address. Significant events like that weave themselves into legend and pass by the lips of traveling merchants and wandering religious mendicants from village to village.

As I saw the *khaddar*-clothed politicians wearing the Gandhi cap driving through different parts of India on electioneering campaigns, I was aware of fresh disturbing forces. The fact that the new constitution gives the vote to perhaps a score of million peasants, out of the thirty-five million male voters, has developed in politicians a new affection for the peasant-farmer. From their own lips I have heard politicians confess with a rather wry smile to the somewhat fantastic promises that they have made under the stress of need for votes. The peasant, who, as we have seen, is economically under intense pressure, has all over British India been promised by politicians of different parties the reduction of rents, the elimination of the landlord, "cheap" money to be loaned at rates far below those of the money-lender, the reduction of taxes, with cheaper and better government-controlled seed, and so on.

[1] A word meaning "Great Soul" and often used by the people as a title of honor for Mr. Gandhi.

The politician comes to the village, pours out his fervid socio-economic propaganda, and goes back to his city environment; but the ideas that he has dropped are like seed that germinates in the mind of the peasant. If poverty becomes even more stringent in village India we may find millions of peasants moving swiftly towards agrarian revolution by their refusal to pay rent or taxes and their repudiation of debts. Pundit Jawaharlal Nehru is, by his own explicit statement, far from being a Communist. But his very drastic socialism, brilliantly expounded in every part of India, blazes the trail for demagogues, less scrupulous than he, ready to capitalize the peasant's material bitterness in the interests of a communistic revolution. The vigorous, well organized left-wing Socialist party in Congress is explicitly Marxian, and in the province of Bihar alone has achieved a membership of one hundred thousand peasants.

The effect on the politician himself is often significant. One of these, an advanced Moslem, freshly back from two weeks' electioneering in villages, said to me, "I have been obliged to change all that I have previously said in electioneering speeches in order to get hold of the peasant. I was obliged to get into very simple Indian dress and had to wade through streams and down boggy roads. I have seen what was to me hitherto unimaginable poverty—families herded under bamboo shanties, with goats, chickens, and all under one roof. Before I talked with them they had no idea of their rights." In this way the new constitution has brought to the door of the peasants politicians who have never cared for them before; while the politicians in turn have had a window opened for them into real conditions in the villages and the titanic potential force that lies relatively latent in the rural millions.

An eminent professor in Hyderabad said to me that the only measure of defense for the government against agitators who foment unrest among ignorant and superstitious villagers is the dissemination of ideas and facts through broadcasting. This is what the state of Hyderabad, as well as that of Mysore, is doing in practice. But this task is extraordinarily complex. There are three different language areas in Hyderabad alone. For this reason language-area broadcasting is undertaken.

Imagine the enormously more complicated problem set to the British government in the task of organizing broadcasting to all British India. In spite, however, of the shackles that are imposed by financial stringency and official timidity, a type of broadcasting program adjusted to the peasant mind has called out remarkable response from village people. Programs in which news about seeds and agricultural pests, health hints and stories, are punctuated by the ever welcome lyrics, have an increasing public in the villages. The number of listeners will increase when the technical problems linked up with securing cheap efficient radios and electrical battery charging are solved. While writing this chapter I have been able to listen in England to a broadcast address from Moscow attacking imperialism in Asia and Europe. These talks, which are given regularly, can be heard in every part of India as clearly as in Britain. Russia has its College of Oriental Students, whose undergraduates and graduates include men speaking most of the languages of India. Italy makes a regular Fascist broadcast from Rome in Hindustani.

There are some six million women voters in India under the new constitution. I suppose that even a decade ago it would have seemed impossible to imagine a Moslem woman candidate for election making a political speech to Moslem village women. Even in 1936 veiled Moslem women shook their fists at Begum Shah Nawaz of Lahore because she appeared unveiled at one of these meetings. This illustrates the vehement opposition toward change that surges in the heart of millions of India's women, Moslem and Hindu. Woman in India is the inner core of the traditional family life. Even when an Indian village woman has, through habitual acquiescence in her husband's judgment, followed him, for instance, into the Christian church, she not infrequently keeps up the secret practice of Hindu rites and hands these on to her children. For this reason any penetration of India with new ideas, Christian or otherwise, is bound to fail unless sustained, skilled approach to the younger womanhood and girlhood of India is organized. "If you lift the woman, the woman will lift the village," says Mr. F. L. Brayne. And Lord Linlithgow writes:

My firm conviction is that no more potent instrument lies to hand for promoting rural development than a bold, determined, persistent drive towards the goal of a sound primary education for the girlhood of the countryside. There, plain for all to see, but hitherto so little apprehended, lies the key, I verily believe, to India's future.[1]

Repeatedly in conversation with groups of students in different colleges and universities of India I asked each one individually to say where his home was. It was startling to find how considerable a proportion came from the villages, and from varied castes in those villages. The student life, then, with which we shall deal later,[2] is definitely a disturbing element in the village. A Christian girls' boarding school, for instance, such as that at Jammalamadugu, finds that the ideas imbibed in studies, the attitudes developed in talks with fellow-students, and the unconscious absorption of new standards of value from the teaching staff, whether Indian or Western, make each of the girls a leavening influence when she returns home. The number of peasant girls so trained who go back into the villages to earn their living as teachers or as nurses bring a startling innovation into the Indian rural pattern, that of the young unmarried woman. Miss D. I. Smith of Jammalamadugu writes:

It is a sign of development that in these days it is possible for a young unmarried girl with an older woman com-

[1] *The Indian Peasant*, by the Marquis of Linlithgow. London, Faber & Faber, 1932.

[2] See Chapter Six.

panion to go and live in our villages and work as a Bible-woman.

A short time ago it was unheard of in rural India that a girl should earn her living as teacher, nurse, or doctor. Today, however, a considerable proportion of the girls from villages who enter boarding schools have training for such a vocation definitely in mind. The many girls from these schools who marry inevitably carry into their home-making, and through their homes into the village, the new ways and attitudes that they have absorbed. Of these, again, a certain number become the wives of Christian pastors or teachers. While rearing their own families, at the same time they take a definite position of leadership in the education of the younger generation of girls. A Western woman who has recently traveled throughout India into large numbers of villages, and has come into touch with many hundreds of different Christian groups, asserts that she can tell at a glance from the appearance and the responsiveness of the women whether or not the village teacher has a trained wife.

It is difficult adequately to express our admiration for the courage and endurance of these trained Christian Indian women in the villages. Often in loneliness, with their husbands traveling to other villages, dreading the many perils that leap like lightning on the Indian victim, exposed to slander, and isolated from the fellowship of kindred minds and spirits, these simple women hold out against the downward tow of a non-Christian environment.

By the quality of their lives and the way they bring up their children, they change the attitudes and standards of many villages. They are the salt of the earth.

III

Looking afresh, then, over village India, we see the age-old rhythm of her life being strangely disturbed by the restless mechanism of the new age and by the ferment of ideas in action, such as nationalism and communism, feminism and Christianity. As we watch this breaking in of new forces our first instinctive action is to throw up our hands in bewilderment. Priceless wealth lies in the old system; untold benefits lie in the new. But the old has cruel shackles; and the new has created evils never dreamed of in the old: world-wide unemployment, the terror of wholesale war-massacre on a scale that makes the wars of the old India sound like picnics. We could not keep the old system if we would; as we count the benefits of the new we would not keep the old as it stands if we could. Yet we should shudder to inflict on the India of tomorrow the menace and the tense strains of the Western world of today.

There are elements of good and of evil in both the old Indian system and in the modern Western system which threatens its existence. Can we discover any guiding principles on which to make our choice of the good in each and our rejection of the evil?

Bolshevism in Russia, taking over an agricultural situation similar in some ways to the Indian, although the old Russian system was feebler and more tenuous, is going out boldly and insistently for swift mechanization of agriculture and the cooperative working of mass farms. Is that what India needs most? Pundit Jawaharlal Nehru says "Yes." Some of the very qualities, however, that Russia must develop if she is to succeed in her task are already fully grown in India. For India, as we have seen, has what Western rural life, most of all in America, tragically lacks —the habit of interdependent specialized service and mutual responsibilities. Two thousand years of Indian life have reposed upon the relative contentment and peace of the peasants. Each man has had his place in the system and his part to play, each supporting the others and receiving support in return. Not only should India conserve that rich possession, but the West should emulate it by all available means. That Western ideas are undermining it in India is illustrated by the advertisement of an Indian insurance company, which reads: "Don't knock at the door of relatives and friends for help and protection in old age. Self-help is the best help. Let us show you how to help yourself."

India, too, has that quality which democratic individualism has tended to destroy in the West—the discipline of the individual to the service of the community. Fascism in Italy or Japan and the Nazi policy of Germany are at root vehement attempts to recover by dictatorship this subordination of the one to the whole which India has quietly developed out of her own life and culture. To throw away that foundation-stone of citizenship in the interests of developing "rugged individualism" and initiative, would be throwing away the baby with the bath water, with a vengeance.

Meanwhile, as we sum up our impressions of the village system, we ask what elements in the life of village India seem to us to be doomed, either by the drive of new life today or by the moral conscience of mankind? Shall we not regard the refusal of equality of opportunity as the root evil of village India? The child of the *dhobi*, of the scavenger, or of the weaver has surely equal rights with the child of the Brahman to the opportunity to learn, or to equip himself for any occupation.

We cannot, however, merely accept equality of opportunity as a principle unless we are prepared to try to develop a pattern of life in India that will provide for the rendering of all the needed services of the village. For the existing order does approximately achieve that goal, although at the price of enforced inequality. The inequality that is integral to the present system springs from the Hindu sacred books and their teaching about the Divine Will. The new equality of opportunity will only come from the Christian teaching of the Divine Will of the Father. Equality of opportunity for unbridled self-expression would spell disaster. The old system of mutual dependence came from the subordination of ranks in a rigid scheme of inequality taught by Hinduism. Can we help a new and living growth of cooperation of equals to spring up in India?

This revolutionary change can result only from the leaven that the hand of Christ is today thrusting into the mass of India. It is rooted in his revelation of the ultimate and priceless value of personality. And, be it observed, that leaven comes not from the West, but from the life and teaching of One who, though universal, was born in Asia, a member of a subject nation under an alien empire.

Chapter Three

A GATEWAY INTO NEW LIFE

I

IN A VILLAGE STREET IN INDIA A MAN PAUSES OUTSIDE A SHOP. Unlike others with red or white lines on their foreheads, he has no such god-marks. His only clothing is a dirty piece of cloth wound round his waist. He stands humbly at some distance and points out to the shopkeeper the goods that he wants. He may not touch them to see what is their quality or thickness. They are not handed to him but are thrown upon the ground for him to pick up, and he leaves the money in payment for them on the ground. He is an outcaste and he must exercise meticulous care not to touch the shopkeeper, who would be defiled by the contact.

He goes down the street and pauses at the entrance to the village shrine to watch the worshippers remove their shoes and pass within. But he must remain outside the gate, where he may worship the god from afar. If he entered the shrine it would be polluted. If he loiters near the door of the school, where his children, however intelligent, will not be admitted, passers-by guard against touching him or being defiled even by his shadow.

He pauses near the well and looks longingly at it, for under the burning sun of India thirst is a cruel torment. Yet he does not approach to draw water, although that well has probably been made by public money for the good of all. He knows his place too well to make the attempt. If any vessel of his touched the water in the well it would be contaminated. So he stands humbly waiting until some person of a higher caste who is charitably inclined draws water and pours it from a height into his water-pot. This will probably happen soon, as merit is acquired by such an act of charity to an outcaste; and in any case the Indian is naturally kindly and friendly.

Some fifty-two million people—equal to more than one-third of the population of the United States—belong to one or another of the many different groups of untouchables, or outcastes, in India. For at least two thousand years they have lived quiescent, subdued, repressed. As with the immense slave-population of ancient Rome, so with the Indian outcaste masses, they bear on their shoulders the burden of the most menial and repulsive labor of the civilization from which they are excluded. Today for the first time those starved shoulders begin to straighten. The outcaste begins to lift his bent head and to open his timid resigned eyes in questioning resentment. Within Hinduism Mr. Gandhi calls for the gates of the temples to be opened to the outcaste. Seeing the betterment of the lives of their fellow-outcastes who have entered the Indian Christian community, these millions of the depressed classes are today going into the church in ever increasing numbers. Even when the pace is slowed down by the stringent demands that we shall examine later,[1] the numbers entering the Christian church have now risen to some fifteen thousand a month and are steadily increasing.

As I look into the face of the Indian outcaste, the picture constantly comes back of the man at the beginning of *The Pilgrim's Progress*, to whom Evangelist says, "You see that wicket gate?" "No," replies the man with the burden on his back. "You see that shining light?" asks the guide, pointing to a more distant horizon. "I think I do," he answers. Seeking that light, he finds the wicket-gate. His quest and its completion fill the rest of the story. The Pilgrim's Progress of the outcaste, which has just started, is India's enigma, a serial story whose chapters still remain to be written.

The removal of untouchability is one of the five planks of the Nationalist party's platform in India. It is also at the heart of both the Good News of Christ and of the program of Christianity there. But the removal of untouchability in India is parallel to the abolition of slavery in America. Standing by itself, liberation acutely intensifies the very problem toward whose solution it tries to contribute. The slave in Alabama was at first in a much worse plight when freed than he had been in the security of the plantation. As a slave he was cared for—however crudely—by a master. He was at least as secure economically as is, say, a

[1] See pp. 54-55.

horse. But, when freed, the slave lost his security; and having been kept ignorant, he was without the capacity to create a new position of his own. The immortality of that freed American slave, Booker T. Washington, rests securely on the fact that he saw that the only way for the Negro to take his true place in the national life was by the development of character and capacity. Booker Washington devoted his life heroically to creating an education that would spiritually, morally, intellectually, and technically equip the Negro for his high destiny.

For the same reason the opening of gates to the Indian outcaste may only exacerbate his agony. To change the mind of Hinduism so that it would open the gate to let the outcaste in would be a miracle. But it would be useless unless the greater miracle were achieved, that he should himself become a new creation. A new spirit must enter into the outcaste that will drive out of him the devils of dependence, inferiority, and insolence, and will lift him out of the drunkenness, dirt, and irresponsibility in which he too often lives. Anyone who has seen a crowd of villagers from the lowest outcaste groups swarming like blowflies on the carcass of a buffalo that has fallen dead, hacking off chunks of carrion and rushing off with them, can hardly escape a deep sense of nausea.

The untouchable is a man to whom Hinduism refuses education, who is dependent on his landlord for his meager livelihood, who is often a serf through perpetual indebtedness. "I am an outcaste," he says. "The gods have said that

I am created to serve the Brahman; that I must live in a hovel away from the dwellings of the caste people." In parts of South India even his shadow is hated for the pollution it spreads. He is avoided as a pestilence. Men would have to go to the priest for purification if he came even within a few paces of them. To have lived under such condemnation from the world creates sheer numbing paralysis. He accepts the verdict. Nowhere in the world is the great word truer than of the outcaste, "Ye must be born again."

II

As I talked with Mr. Gandhi about his sustained campaign for bringing the untouchables into the fold of Hinduism I realized afresh how much heroic sacrificial service Hindus working with his organization, the Harijan Sevak Sangh, are rendering to the depressed classes. One great contribution of Mr. Gandhi's own thought and policy lies in his piercing insight into the fact that untouchability works havoc not simply in the untouchable but in those who regard him as such. His view is closely parallel to that of Booker T. Washington with regard to the white man and the Negro. Washington was never tired of repeating, "If you are going to hold a man down in the ditch you have to stay down in the ditch with him." That, however, is not all. For a great Indian Christian to whom I quoted this saying replied, "Yes, but if you are going to raise the man from the ditch, you must also first go down into the ditch where he is, in order to pull him out."

The fierce implacable resentment of orthodox Hinduism against lifting the untouchables is illustrated in the reactions during 1937 to the opening in 1936 of temples in Travancore to outcastes. The resistance was so great that the entrance of the outcastes was limited to special hours; and the Maharajah's government ordered the gift of thirty rupees a day to each of such temples for purification ceremonies after the outcastes departed, to "cleanse" the temple for the ordinary caste worshippers. The abstention of caste worshippers from visiting these temples was so pronounced that the government issued orders to Hindu officials that they must go to the temples for worship.

Leading Brahmans from Travancore went to a famous Hindu *guru* (spiritual leader), who is called His Holiness the Swamy of the Sri Sringeri Mutt, to ask his pronouncement regarding the temples into which the untouchables had been permitted to penetrate. His reply was that the spirit of the god had left those temples because they were defiled. "They are no longer temples," he said. Extend that pronouncement to cover Hinduism all over India and you begin to have some glimmering of the Himalayan task that such resistance creates for the relatively small body of Hindu reformers.

Those early laws of over two thousand years ago that established untouchability and the perpetuation of it through the centuries give a man practically no fulcrum from within Hinduism with which to lever untouchability out of the religion. And those laws still govern the general popular mind of Hinduism and the convictions of its most potent Brahman intellectual leaders. With Christianity the situation is precisely reversed. If we find caste or class divisions inside the Christian church, we know that they exist in flat defiance of the acts and the teaching of Christ. They war against his revelation of the nature and will of God.

In a conversation with Mr. Gandhi I asked him what his authority is in religion. He tapped on his breast with his fingers and said, "It is here"; and he went on to say that every scripture must ultimately come to the test of a man's own inner reason and conscience. Gandhi is ready therefore to defy, if necessary, the scriptures of Hinduism. As he has written, "I shall not make a fetish of religion and I cannot justify any evil in its sacred name. I have no desire to carry one single soul with me if I cannot convince him by an appeal to his reason. I shall even go to the length of rejecting the divinity of the most ancient Shastras, if they do not appeal to my reason." He said to me, however, that the only scripture of any religion that was to him faultless was the Bhagavad-Gita, that beautiful philosophical poem which conveys its pantheistic teaching in song form.

Mr. Gandhi then attacked with some warmth the work of Christians in India, and especially the bringing of the Harijans within the fold of the Christian church. Harijan means "the offspring of God" and is the word used by Gandhi as a general title for the outcaste people. When Hinduism is reforming itself, he argued, it is not "playing the game" for Christians in India to intensify their efforts. I might have pointed out to Mr. Gandhi that that is very far from the truth today. For the most heart-breaking problem that confronts the Christian community in India, whether missionary or national, is that the multitudes of depressed-class groups from villages who are knocking at the door of the church asking to be allowed to come in are overwhelmingly greater than the numbers with whom the church, under her present system of working, is able to deal.

Leaving that issue aside I asked Mr. Gandhi: "Do you not think that, to a considerable extent, the sacrificial work of Christians over many years has led, on the one hand, to stirrings within Hinduism of interest and sympathy for the Harijans, and, on the other, to many millions of the depressed classes entering the Christian community or feeling the stirring of desire for freedom and a better life?"

Mr. Gandhi agreed that there was truth in this analysis. I could not then refrain from wondering whether it was just or reasonable to ask those Christians who had been the main cause of this awakening of social conscience in India to fold their tents and leave at the very hour when so many hands were being stretched out for their help. It is to be regretted that he has never (in spite of repeated invitations) visited the Christian village churches nor seen the transformation that has actually come into the lives of millions of depressed-class people through their entrance into the Christian community of India.

III

It is beyond question that the outcastes in coming to the Indian pastor to ask for knowledge of the Christian way of life are prompted by a blend of motives. Watching the Christian groups around him, the animist outcaste sees that their houses become cleaner, their backs lose the cringing stoop and their eyes the glint of dread. The giving up of toddy not only clears the brain but makes for economy. The money-lender's grip loosens on the Christian outcaste. The folk who once tremblingly bowed before a stone stained with the blood of a cockerel or cowered before the smallpox goddess, now as Christians become the joint creators of a house of God. Even though that sanctuary may be built of thatch and mud, it radiates dignity; and daily those once terror-stricken animists make it resound with joyful praises of the God of love.

For the outcastes the ultimate horizon of life is the village. When they see in neighboring villages changes such as we have just described, these become a constant subject of debate around the village fires at night. The improvement that they see is economic and esthetic, hygienic and spiritual—all inextricably interwoven. If to respond to a call sounded by that improved way of living is to come under the charge of mixed motives, which of us is immune? Moreover, what higher call are the outcastes psychologically capable of hearing, even if, as is not the case, any purer spiritual note had ever sounded in their ears? If we ask for evidence of the reality of this improvement we hear it from the lips of multitudes of Hindu caste people who have now, as we shall show, come under its spell.

How does this change work in the life of the individual? Anyone who has lived in the villages could cite many cases like one that, among others, came my way while traveling in India. A caste man, a Hindu, ill-treated a Christian outcaste boy so violently and continuously for having made some blunder that the youth had to be taken to a hospital. Shortly afterwards the caste Hindu himself was converted to Christianity. A year later the village landlord began to attack brutally the mother of this same boy for not running to him at once when ordered to his house. She was looking after her sick child and could not leave him. The caste man, who a year before had beaten the Christian boy, now stood up to protect that outcaste boy's mother from persecution, saying to the landlord: "You shall not ill-treat her, we both belong now to the Christian brotherhood."

The matter goes deeper than we have yet suggested. What is given to the outcaste who comes into the Christian fold today is never economic betterment but the power to raise himself. Something priceless is breathed into his very personality, so that there springs up in him an irresistible desire to make the environment about him correspond to the cleaner heart within, and he is given at the same time the capacity to brace himself for the effort. Working in the Christian villages of the depressed classes the Indian and the European worker alike are often sick at heart. Railing and reviling, bestiality and chicanery, grossness and every form of backsliding can be found. In a word, every one of the almost unmentionable vilenesses that form St. Paul's catalogue of the sins of the Galatians, Corinthians, and other early Christians are there in the primitive Indian church. It is therefore perhaps as well for us to remember that the early church, about which all the Pauline condemnations were true, was the mother-church of us all. And, indeed, when we come to ponder the Christian ethical standards which shine in the Sermon on the Mount and radiate from the parables of the Good Samaritan and of the Sheep and the Goats, and if we examine our Western Christendom, infected with class-consciousness and pride, economic acquisitiveness and censorious judgment, we are brought to the place where we must kneel alongside the outcaste church and say, "We have all sinned and come short of the glory of God."

What does stand out as incontrovertible is, first, that every month at least fifteen thousand outcastes are coming out of animism to enter the church in India because of the changed lives of their fellow-men who are of the Christian fold. Second, the one thing really given to the outcaste is a new heart that is itself the source of his own betterment. "The outcaste," as one of the greatest Indian leaders said to me, "does not come into the Christian church for the loaves and fishes, for we have no loaves and fishes to give him."

IV

Are there many more baffling and testing decisions to make than that of the Indian pastor and the Western missionary who today, face to face with scores of thousands of ignorant men and women who have caught a glimpse of a new way of life, must refuse or permit their admission to the Christian fold? To lower standards of Christian living out of pity is natural, but calamitous; for the outcome is a baptized heathenism. This unfortunately does exist in parts of India. Yet to impose any test based on Western standards of value (which are more largely founded on the Roman law of property and Stoic principles than on the Sermon on the Mount), in a word, to set any test that contains elements that Christ does not require, excludes from the church visible those whom he would admit.

Confronted with this vital issue, Indian and Western Christians from all parts of India were brought together in December, 1936, by the National Christian Council of India, Burma and Ceylon[1] to try to frame some principles and standards, and to consider methods of dealing with

[1] See p. 156.

groups of people who desire to become Christians and to receive Christian instruction.

What, first of all, are the standards needed for entrance into the church? In a word, what requirements must be fulfilled before baptism? The goal was defined as "nothing less than a conscious individual relationship with Christ as Savior from sin, and Lord in every relationship of life." A regular practice of individual, family, and congregational worship is essential to a growing experience and enjoyment of fellowship with God. "To develop a Christian conscience in the people which shall bring about the transformation of all social relationships by a growing acceptance of the ethical implications of the Christian way of life," was set up as a further objective.

Such high planes are obviously remote from the existing life of these outcastes on their bewildered quest. Experienced workers therefore outlined practical means of attaining these aims.

An act of enrollment is the first step. Those desiring to become Christian give their names and those of the members of their family who wish to be enrolled, promising to cease idol worship and to go to the Christian pastor or the Bible-woman to learn the elements of the faith. Here we come face to face with the first fundamental problem of dealing with the multitudes in these group movements—the provision of enough Christian Indian pastors and teachers qualified to give the knowledge and to radiate the contagious spirit of the Christian life.

A simple practical step of high value is taken when a group of perhaps five or six families asking for knowledge of the Way provide a little house in which a pastor-teacher and his wife can come to live. In one place that I visited in Tinnevelly the villagers were beginning work that very day on the little mud-and-thatch structure that was to be for them the house of God.

At an early stage in this first process a service of admission into the catechumenate is found valuable. In that ceremony people make a definite public promise to give up evil practices, including the drinking of toddy, and to adopt Christian ways of conduct, including Christian rules of marriage, ways of mutual help, and the filling of the Lord's Day with positive content. What is vital here is not so much prohibition as positive dynamic guidance into the adventurous Christian way.

Obviously no merely sporadic teaching or occasional pastoral care is adequate for this continuous educational process. For the very life pattern of largely adult groups has to be changed. If people coming from this background are to be trained for sturdy Christian life and service, sustained teaching is essential. This is true to the very earliest experience of the church as recorded in the beginning of Acts in relation, for instance, to Antioch, where Paul and Barnabas spent at least a year, we are told, in continuous teaching of the newly gathered church. The lack of this continuous development by the teacher-pastor and his wife living and working among the people is the primary cause of the lamentable paganism and the fathomless ignorance of Christ and his teaching still to be found among many baptized outcaste groups. The "seven devils" of Indian secular life—chicanery, log-rolling, backbiting, impurity, scandal, caste-arrogance, and even lobbying for election—have, on the testimony of Indians themselves, still to be cast out of many of their churches and church councils.

In a quickened sense of responsibility among the rank and file of young laymen and women in the more advanced Indian churches lies the solution of this problem. Wherever we find them giving themselves to leadership among underprivileged groups of Christian peasants, we see the church move forward with a fresh resilience.

One reason why the leadership of educated young laymen springing from caste families is so helpful is the paralyzing situation in which the Christian outcaste leader of outcastes finds himself. Face to face with Hindu caste people the man of outcaste birth eternally sees in their faces their sense of his inferiority. Face to face with his own fellow-outcastes the leader is haunted by their blend of submissiveness with insolence. This is a characteristic of peasant leadership of peasants everywhere. Nervous irritability rises against one who in brain and standing has risen above the ruck of his fellows. His very capacities stimulate herd antagonism. Face to face with the missionary, the Christian Indian outcaste leader is often torn between two warring impulses. The first is to resent and resist the sense of white superiority which the missionary honestly denies. Yet superiority is so ingrained within the Westerner that only by a miracle of grace can he rise above it. The second impulse of the outcaste leader is to be submissive to and imitative of the missionary. Both are evil.

These psychological factors are enough to account for the lack of initiative, absence of creative enterprise, and failure to achieve spiritual adventure, which in the Indian Christian community are frequently the despair of the missionary. The best of men are thus caught in a vicious circle. The Indian church leader awaits the missionary's initiative. The missionary, irritated at the inertia, becomes convinced that no enterprise will be launched without his, the white man's, drive. All of us who are honest know the profound and subtle antipathies that spring up in us against those who persistently sap our energies. So white men may wake to discover with horror that contempt or hate has sprung up within them against the very flock whom they have given up all to serve. No spiritual cooperation can live where there is concealed resentment. The relation of the white missionary and the Indian can be poisoned at the springs by the profound instincts within Indian nationalism and white imperialism. Nothing short of rebirth into the one "household of God" can create deeply satisfying, fruitful unity of spirit between men culturally, racially, and nationally alien from one another. This miracle is gloriously happening all over the map of India.

Pursuing the aim of creating a united, radiant Christian community out of underprivileged and grossly ignorant outcastes, the National Christian Council followed up the program already outlined by the following minimum scheme of teaching: (a) an outline of the life of our Lord Jesus Christ; (b) teaching on God, the Father, the Son, and the Holy Ghost, and on the church; (c) the laws of Christian conduct, founded on the Ten Commandments interpreted by the New Testament; and (d) instruction about the sacraments of baptism and of the Lord's Supper. High value is set on memorizing central parts of Christian teaching, such as the Lord's Prayer, some passages from the Scriptures, and the creeds (where they are in use).

There should be a constant emphasis upon regular worship, with the enrichment that comes from the lifting up of the heart in thanksgiving and adoration and from confession, intercession, and the reading from the Bible. In the services of worship silent meditation should break the singing or saying of responses, while the spoken common recital of covenants, the thrill of praise through action song or drama, and especially the development of children's song and recital and action, bring into play the talent of Indian Christian poets and musicians, who are called to create lyrics that will quicken as well as express our many-sided Christian experience. These are all integral to the creation of outcaste groups into living Christian communities, a part of the catholic church throughout the world. Already the village people in different parts of India enjoy indigenous ways of worship and have created lyrics to be sung while working in the fields, and action songs which, although they are not generally known, yet if shared all over India would bring new color and radiance to the common life of the Christian peasants and stir them to lively spiritual adventure in spreading the gospel story through music and drama, social service and preaching.

How, the National Christian Council again asked, can these churches with so crude a background sustain the distinctive sacredness of the life of the church? Rigid censoriousness would make cruel demands. The imposition of tests that overemphasize moral laws of secondary importance is dangerous. To lift the standard of life without pharisaism calls for the highest exercise of imaginative insight. That insight must be both into the mind of Christ and into the life of the outcaste.

Where serious and sustained offense against the Christian standard of life prevails in a man or a group, the National Christian Council advocates personal inquiry by a responsible representative of the church, followed by more public inquiry carried out by the *panchayat*.[1] In this way guilt is assessed and discipline decided. The goal throughout is repentance, reformation, and restoration. Laxity which leads to drunkenness, reviling, extortion, and impurity is prevented when strong friendly Christian workers make contact with these infant congregations of primitive people as they take their first stumbling steps along the Christian way.

[1] See pp. 18-20.

Here again the heart of progress lies in bringing more and better workers, Indian and missionary, professional and lay, into the work of building up the village church. One wholehearted Western missionary, ready to rough it and "endure hardness" in comradeship with Indian Christians, can do glorious work in this way. To take a single example from life today, I think of one woman missionary who has recently been dedicated to such work. She develops summer schools, organizes retreats for the wives of evangelists and Christian women, and invents continually new experimental approaches to the people in their homes and fields in an area having a total population of half a million. Here, scattered through three hundred and eighty-two villages, is a newly baptized community of twenty thousand Christians. For the greater part of the time she lives in camp, moving from center to center over that huge area. Such a life may terrify the timid and exhaust the anemic; but for courageous, full-blooded womanhood at once courteous and comradely, here lies a path of adventure for the Kingdom.

In these great tasks the Christian man and woman must go to the people in need as Christ came to men and "dwelt among them." The call is to go into the village and share the common life of the people. The young Indian teacher-pastor and his wife, living in their simple home, and bringing up their children there, manifest the Christian life to the villager in the place where the villager himself has to try to be a Christian.

V

It is tormenting not to be able to take the reader personally through those remote villages that are the true India that no tourist knows. A scene comes up before me of a long hot afternoon on the banks of a stream, with the sunlight throwing mottled light and shadow through the palm-leaf thatch of an improvised *pandal.* Squatted on the ground all down the length of the shade were hundreds of peasants of the depressed classes. They had been under instruction in their villages for from six months to a year on the lines described above. Now they had come for baptism. Young men and women and the aged came together. Mothers were baptized and then held up their babies for baptism, as the minister in charge and his assistants went on hour after hour with the sacrament in that tremendous heat. Grouped round outside were interested watchers taking in the scene that for these reverent villagers was opening the door into a new community.

From the *pandal* I went on toward a crossroads where the resident Indian pastor met us and led us through a Christian village with its clusters of mud-walled, cleanly homes thatched with palm leaves. In the faces of the men and women, and most of all in those of the boys and girls, I saw a radiance that escapes the net of words. It shines from the glowing sense of liberation that comes as the gift of Christ when in him they see the face of a Father who banishes the terror of the cholera goddess and other demons.

These Christians led me proudly to an enormous ridge of bricks. In that ridge were eighty thousand bricks that these villagers themselves with their own hands had molded and baked. They had toiled in their spare time to make this material to build a new church to house their growing membership. They wished a house of God worthy of the Lord whom they worshipped. They had also raised hundreds of rupees themselves from their slender resources. But they wanted help from the West to buy timber for the roof. Every element in that picture is a symbol of Christianity in India. It is really rooted in the life of the people. They themselves give money to build an Indian church; but they must also have the cooperation of the West.

That this remote group of outcastes should have had not only the impulse but the steady sustained industry sufficient to achieve that task, is a psychological and spiritual miracle. To leave them to stagger on with all the burden on their shoulders is as cruel as it is unreasonable.

I was then taken into the existing church whose inadequacy was a matter of great concern to the people. The wall of the church was some four feet high, of sun-dried mud. Trunks of palm-trees in the center upheld the ridge-pole, from which sloped down on either side the palm-thatch roof. This roof was carried out over the edge of the mud wall on either side. A foot or more of open space between the top of the wall and the roof let breezes blow into the church. As the congregation sat on the floor there and sang with an infectious lilt the Indian Christian lyrics, we shared a spiritual experience that, on the one hand, was a gift that Indian and Westerner had received from on high, and, on the other, demonstrated the insignificance and irrelevance of differences of race or color or culture in the world fellowship of Christ's disciples.

A few weeks later, within the still unfinished walls of the cathedral being built at Dornakal, the village people from far and wide came together for their harvest thanksgiving. The immaculate usher taking up in stately dignity the offering of a Western bourgeois congregation would have been startled if asked to share in taking up this collection. Men staggered up the aisle bearing large bags of rice weighing as much as two hundred pounds. That rice was not bought in sacks from a merchant. It represented a twentieth of the crop from Christian villages. Those sacks of rice were gifts in addition to the weekly contributions of handfuls of rice set aside for the service of God from the sparse daily supper of the poor peasant-farmer and his family. The flutterings of agitated birds stirred the congregation as two or three hundred hens were brought up to the altar. One of them announced her own contribution to the collection by exultant cluckings as she laid a ceremonial thanksgiving egg. Goats, lambs, and piles of fruit and grain from which the eager muzzles of calves had to be restrained, made up a never-to-be-forgotten offering by the poor to the work of God.

It would be literally true to say that in proportion to income these offerings meant far more in sheer sacrifice than the impressive money gifts of a Western suburban congregation. The old facile chatter about "rice Christians" that one hears is not simply a vague excusable misstatement; it is a wicked and stupid slander. They are certainly "rice Christians," but only in the lovely sense revealed in those sacks of sacrificial offerings.

Is there any stranger irony in the Indian scene than that the men of lower and middle caste—the group of craftsmen and farmers who are the real backbone of India—should after all these years be entering the Christian community, led, not by the missionary or by the converted Brahman, but by the witness of the life of the outcaste? If anyone ten years ago had prophesied what we now see he would have been derided as a fantastic optimist. During the last decade tens of thousands of craftsmen and farmers of these central castes have come to the leaders of the Christian church in India asking for teaching. When the question is put to them, "What leads you to come to us?" the reply is that they have seen the changes in the lives of the depressed classes.

Dr. Azariah, Bishop of Dornakal, tells in a letter of an experience that illuminates this fresh and momentous development. He was about to conduct a confirmation service for a Christian church gathered from the depressed classes. The fifty members were seated on the ground, but the Bishop saw a group of Hindu caste men seated on a bench. He asked them to leave as he was about to conduct a service for the Christians. They moved but really only ranged themselves behind Dr. Azariah, unknown to him. After the service was over the caste people still waited and he spoke to the headman, saying that he was glad to see them. The caste man said, "The fathers of these men were the serfs of our fathers. Their parents have been working for my parents for years and years. Who are they? They are not superior to us in caste, they are not superior to us in looks, but as I was standing there looking at them I felt that the light of the great God came to rest on their faces. There is a glory, there is a joy which we have not got. Now I want you to come and tell my people what Christianity can do for them."

Curiously enough, this peasant-farmer had put his finger upon the central source of the improved life of the outcaste. The scientific researches carried through with meticulous accuracy and inexhaustible energy by that scholarly and practical American pioneer, Bishop J. Waskom Pickett, and published in that invaluable volume, *Christian Mass Movements in India*, reveal that the cause of the flowing tide of Indian peasants into the church is, to repeat it once again, the demonstration given by men and women who are living the Christian life in the village street, as did their Master. Their supreme source of strength is found in that central fellowship where men extend the open palm to take the Bread of Life, and each man feeds on Christ in his heart with thanksgiving.

Chapter Four

STRIKING DEEP ROOTS

I

Seated on a veranda absorbed in talk with a gifted Indian Christian, Archdeacon Subbayya, I caught the sound of singing coming from a neighboring hilltop. My absorption in Mr. Subbayya's talk was due not only to his radiant personality, but to the fact that he revealed a range of Christian leadership that I had never met before in any land. He is simultaneously dramatist, lyrical poet, author, musician, orator, and pilgrim-pastor and teacher, moving constantly from village to village, inspiring men not only with deep feeling and enthusiasm but with stirring projects for adventurous new activity.

Born of Christian Telugu parents, he distinguished himself as a boy at boarding school by being so persistently full of mischief that the missionary in charge felt obliged to dismiss him from the school. He ran away to another school where his exuberant energies fitted him to be trained as a teacher. He took a teaching post in a girls' school, and married. The Reverend V. S. Azariah (now Bishop of Dornakal) got Dr. Sherwood Eddy to join with him in holding evangelistic meetings at Bezwada. Young Subbayya came a five days' journey by river boat (at two miles an hour) to attend the meetings. His heart was "strangely warmed," and the personal experience of the grace of God that came to him then has remained with him and sustains a persistent flame of inventive enthusiasm for the advancement of the kingdom of God. He prepared for ordination.

As I talked with him on his veranda he had in his hands proofs of the last pages of a book then being printed, into which he has concentrated the variegated fruits of his years of initiative in expressing through Indian modes of expression, in action and in thought, the gospel that it is his joy to radiate.

How illuminating to Western Christians that book would be if translated from the original Telugu into English! A double light would spring from it. First, the West would have a fresh ray of insight into the heart of the Indian Christian community in its expanding activity. Second, they would surely get new practical ideas for their own work in the West. The book begins with hints to village evangelists on how to preach, what to preach, and how to answer questions, with a discussion on the importance of preaching. Mr. Subbayya goes on to give in outline some addresses for Hindus on God's love, and the meaning of eternal life, always presenting the gospel in its central simplicity and not drawing hostile contrasts with Hinduism—such as the contrast between the Christian teaching on sin and the doctrine of *karma.* When Archdeacon

Subbayya himself is preaching he draws pictures as he preaches, with colored crayons. This practice he commends to those who can draw.

Outline notes now follow on talks adapted specially for women, for young men, for old men, for children; with special attention to the great days of the Christian Year—Good Friday, Easter Sunday, Christmas Day and so on. He also lists pertinent proverbs useful in driving home ideas to village people, and sayings collected by him from English books; to which he adds stories and anecdotes that he has found useful, classified under headings.

Christian song and drama are Mr. Subbayya's most lively and original gift to India. They fill the next part of his book, which is extensive. It contains, first, lyrics on the life of Christ and on his parables; lyrics, for instance, that women can sing as they are planting rice or grinding grain; or for use at Christian weddings. The Indian will always sing; and until these Christian lyrics come to them they necessarily sing Hindu songs. Ballads on the gospel, with suggestions for their rendering with musical instruments, follow. He also gives the outline of three *kalakshepams*,[1] or chanted stories, from Scripture, interspersed with spoken explanations and hints on how to start the village people themselves singing in rhythmic forms such thoughts on the gospel.

As an ordinand, Mr. Subbayya responded to a suggestion to write a drama on Amos by producing an eighty-

[1] The word *kalakshepam* really means "whiling away time."

page manuscript in Telugu. This threw into vivid dramatic form as complete an exposition of the life and teaching of Amos as anything in English. He followed this up with one on Jeremiah. They are both enormously successful among village Christian groups and are used widely in other areas than the Telugu field. The nearest approach to a parallel in English would be to think of the swing and lilt of Gilbert and Sullivan opera, combined with the devotional glow and intimate fellowship with Christ that burns in all Archdeacon Subbayya's activity, and—as it burns—makes something quite new.

The Queen of Sheba may strike the Western mind as an unlikely subject for an evangelistic drama. Mr. Subbayya proves that such a judgment is hopelessly wrong. Taking the words of Christ that the Queen of Sheba "came from the ends of the earth to hear the wisdom of Solomon; and behold, a greater than Solomon is here," his drama begins in the Abyssinian court of the Queen. Declaring that she is going to sail up the Red Sea from Abyssinia to Palestine, she is beset by the clamor of her maidens as to the peril and the uselessness of such a departure from the security and the luxury of her court. The Queen, however, describes the marvelous wisdom of Solomon and declares that she must go to imbibe that knowledge. So she sets out on her journey. A kind of Greek chorus then demands, in a sequence of dramatic questions, Since we have access to One before whose wisdom that of Solomon pales, and if the

Queen of Sheba would brave all these dangers to find Solomon, what should not we do to brush aside all difficulties that may hinder us from going to Christ?

In the second act, when the Queen is at Solomon's court, the tense scene depicting the King's judgment about the two mothers and the baby works peasant audiences to fever-heat until Solomon's judgment is given. In this dramatic act are lawyers, pleaders, witnesses, soldiers, the women and the baby, making a grand scene into which the village Christians throw themselves with self-forgetting zest. The chorus then comes in with the presentation of the wonderful judgments of Christ and the question, Is it not all-important that we should go to him whose judgments are full of wisdom? The drama moves to a final description by a speaker of Christ on his throne, which is the Cross. The hands that blessed the children, gave food to the hungry, and healed the sick are pierced; yet he cries, "Father, forgive them."

The author told me how he first experimented with this drama with a group of Christian peasant craftsmen and farmers as the actors. The local *zamindar*, or landlord, a non-Christian, said that he would cover all expenses if the group would act it in his courtyard. He sent for all his relatives, who packed the courtyard, while the *zenana* women crowded the terrace above, with wives of other rich men of the neighborhood. When they had been listening for three hours enthralled, a Hindu government officer stood up and made a speech saying, "Come and preach to us like that and we will listen for any length of time."

An Indian teacher came to the Archdeacon asking, "Can you not give me a lyric that my Christians can sing as they plant the grain?" He did so, and its use spread widely, so that now Christians sing this lyric in the fields at their work. A Hindu landlord, hearing the singing, sent for the teacher to call all the workers into the marketplace. The teacher-pastor led them as they sang to the landlord and the non-Christian villagers.

So we recall the sound of singing which I heard coming down from the hill-top as I talked to Archdeacon Subbayya. It was a stormy afternoon moving toward sunset when we climbed the hill. Owing to a thunderstorm an open-air children's service had been canceled; but we found that some seventy boys, refusing to be robbed of their sing-song, were seated in a circle with an older leader. They asked what I would like them to do.

"Ask them to sing an action song," I suggested. The boys, laughing, asked the Archdeacon to teach them a new one. He called ten boys to him, and forming them in a circle with himself, they went round and round singing in their own language:

Let us go to Calvary,
Do not say the way is hard or long.
(And the hands were stretched out ahead.)
Let us go to Calvary.

So the song went on, he teaching and they learning.

What shall we find when we get there?
The crown of thorns upon his head,
The pierced hands and the pierced feet.
(And their hands went to their heads, and then pointed to their feet.)
Let us go to Calvary.

Then they came to the last verse:

What shall we find there?
Freedom and joy and peace.
Let us go to Calvary.

Archdeacon Subbayya then stepped out of the circle and choosing one of the boys said, "Now you lead them."

Within twenty minutes not only had those boys learned a new Christian action song but they had been trained to teach it to other boys.

We have concentrated on this one narrative to give clearly a local picture of a vigorous type of development of profoundly Indian modes of presenting the gospel—modes that are being taken up eagerly by the church. Other examples could be cited from Travancore, Tinnevelly, Medak, or even among aboriginal hill-tribes, like the Bhils, in remote places in different parts of India.

The *kalakshepam*, already mentioned, is also used as a lively form of witness. Here the leader will sing for a little, accompanied by the drum and one or two other instruments. Then he will explain, in dramatic form, with the help of a few assistants, the story he has sung, which may be, for instance, the women at the Tomb, the exiles in Babylon, or some scenes from *The Pilgrim's Progress.* The wandering minstrel groups of the European Middle Ages afford a parallel.

As I listened to the people in the villages singing their Christian songs in the cool shadow of their church, not only in their own tongue but in their own musical modes, and singing them with rhythm and abandon, with handclapping and faces aglow, I realized that it is sheer nonsense to criticize missions on the ground that they are leading these Oriental people into a Western faith. They sing in Indian words, to Indian music, the praises of the universal God, revealed to them through One born on the soil of Asia.

The inventive experiments now going on in Indian ways of expression are a really great contribution to the central issue of evangelistic witness. When a Subbayya teaches the women at the handmill to sing Christian lyrics in place of Hindu songs as they work, he is incidentally making them missionaries. When a leader competent in the use of Indian forms takes his little choir out into the marketplace of a country town and there, drawing out his violin, begins to sing his Christian *bhajans,* which are lyrical narratives of the gospel story or of the parables, he is achieving two results of outstanding value. As the market crowds listen for hours on end and join in the choruses, the evangelist is deepening the grasp of the

Indian upon his gospel and of the gospel upon him by weaving thought and action into one. Second, he is using a medium, that of dramatic lyric, through which for centuries the Indian has absorbed his religious knowledge. Ancient India has transmitted all her knowledge through poetry, whether history or even grammar.

Christian worship or celebration sometimes takes the form not of an entirely original conception but of an adaptation of a Hindu practice. For instance, in the Medak district of Hyderabad State, it is a custom at one of the Hindu festivals to put cone-shaped baskets upside down on the ground and fill the interstices with flowers; then the girls dance round them singing Hindu lyrics. Among the more than one hundred thousand Christians in the villages of Medak today, the maidens put on their best saris and carry little lights in their hands as they dance in the evening round baskets of flowers singing Christian songs.

Every Hindu temple has a *bhajan-sangha*, or music group. The village churches far and wide are developing Christian *bhajan-sanghas* of young people. They do wonderful natural evangelism. One of their lovely customs is to go on Sunday in procession through the village singing the congregation to church. It is glorious to see the people come out as the youths pass and join the procession, and then to watch them enter singing into their little thatched church.

The thrilling experience every Easter in Medak illuminates the function of a majestic church of cathedral dimensions that rises in real beauty on a commanding hillcrest.[1] The mission has been subject to criticism for permitting the erection of so expensive a church, even though a great part of its cost was covered by the gifts of interested individuals in the West. Those who make this criticism, claiming among other things that the village folk are not able to maintain such an elaborate plant, would surely get new light if they could be there at some such time as Easter. From all sides, in thousands upon thousands, the Christians move from long distances, as far as a hundred miles away, toward the center where the church is. Boys go out into the jungle and bring back palm branches, into which their sisters stick bright red flowers. So armed they march upon the church after going round and round the villages, waving their palms and singing, "Victory, victory, victory today." They pour into the church with palms waving and voices chanting. Quite literally, "The tribes go up to the house of God." And it is their own house of God, for each village, even each person, is conscious of having put aside the regular handful of rice to go toward its building.

Each little group go back to their own village from these thrilling services knowing, out of the most vivid and moving experience of their lives, that they are part of a great community whose worship centers in a lovely

[1] A picture of this church will be found on p. 79 of *Heritage of Beauty*, by Daniel J. Fleming. New York, Friendship Press, 1937.

temple, the glory of which no Hindu shrine or Moslem mosque can outshine. The lift thus given to depressed-class Christians still half terrified by the sheer might of the Hinduism from which they have so recently escaped is of incalculable value. That church on the hill, to whose building their own gifts have contributed, stands for the one thing in the life of these Christians that towers above caste differences between Hindus, and above race differences. It bridges, too, the distinction between governors and governed, and brings men and women together in equal fellowship. All those things constitute a social as well as a spiritual revolution. At all times such a witness would be vital in India; but today, when the old order begins to go to pieces and when traditional loyalties are losing their once unquestioned authority, we hail with joy every building or organization, as well as every educational and social process, that can make clearer the outlines of the church that is above all distinctions of race, nation, sex, or class.

The growing Indian church receives a thrill of joy and is braced for new advance, also, when it dramatizes its own story and looks back to its tiny beginnings. In 1937, for instance, there was held in Ludhiana the centennial of the founding of the Presbyterian mission there by the heroic pioneer, John Lowrie, who reached his post after months of hard travel, in the course of which he lost his wife and companions by death on the road. In a sequence of scenes forming a striking pageant the Punjabi Christians enacted the successive advances of that century, not only with impressive effect on their Moslem and Hindu audiences, but also with encouragement and new determination in their own hearts. The church that grew out of these small beginnings in Ludhiana is now part of the United Church of Northern India, with five synods, over a thousand organized churches, seventy-seven thousand communicants, and a quarter of a million non-communicant adherents.

Another exhilarating moving picture stirs the pulse as we look at the range of influence of one village of depressed-class "down-and-outs" in whose lives Christ has worked transformation. As we read the bald record in the following sentences are we not indeed wading knee-deep in miracle? Many years ago American missionaries went on evangelistic tours and called at Dedgaon in the Marathi area of North India. The caste people scorned the preaching. Those who listened to it were the illiterate outcastes. They asked for a school for their children. Gradually a church was developed that learned to read; it began to evangelize other villages. At least one hundred and fifty men and women from the Christian group have gone out into India as teachers, industrial workers, carpenters, masons, railway officials, and government servants. One man, who went to America, graduated at Bowdoin College and Bangor Seminary and became pastor of the largest church in western India. Another took American training that equipped him to go back as a doctor and eye specialist in a great city. A third, whose father was born and brought up in that village church, after graduating at Andover Seminary and taking his M.A. and Ph.D. at Harvard, became professor of psychology and philosophy in one of India's most famous Christian colleges, and president both of the All-India Conference of Indian Christians and of the Philosophical Association of All India. This village church at Dedgaon, with its four hundred members, belongs to a church council made up of Church of Scotland, Methodist, and American Congregationalist mission churches, and is a part of the United Church of Northern India.

II

Many missionaries and Indian Christians reading these lines will say, either with questioning in their minds or simply out of their own disheartenment, that no such growth of initiative and expanding radiation has come within their own experience where they work and live in India. This we may well expect in a land of European dimensions: you might, for instance, in Europe have a great revival in Scandinavia while the Balkans were left unmoved. It is also true everywhere that second and third generation Christians do show a tendency to become formal and habitual rather than eager and radiant in their faith. An inherited tradition is rarely as vivid as an original experience that has driven a man to take a decisive stand in face of hostile forces. Even in places, however, where second generation Christianity has lost its first momentum, there is often a slow maturing of the Christian conscience. As a woman who lives among them in India pointed out to me, "The whole level of their lives has been almost unconsciously lifted until, when some big moral issue arises, their automatic response to it is almost sure to be based on Christian standards." When this has happened, Christianity is really rooted in Indian soil.

The tragic condition of many little Christian groups in India, especially in the north where they have been baptized into the church and then left for long periods virtually without any shepherding or teaching from missionary or teacher-pastor, emphasizes the crying need for sustained, patient, zealous teaching and training in the regular practice of congregational worship. The alternative is what we find all too frequently in parts of India, a baptized Hinduism or, still worse, animism.

The church in India, as in the West, has far to go. It is vital, first of all, that the local congregation should realize its own unity. But unfortunately in all too many churches in India caste still has some hold, either dividing the Christians within the church, as notably in some Roman Catholic congregations, or operating by the exclusion of other castes from the church. All too often, again, the Christian community in India has automatically tended to think of its own task as being centered within its own walls, the missionary alone being responsible for evangelistic extension. This has, in the past, been due rather to the policy of mission boards in the West than to any fault in the Indian church itself. The Indian Christian community—like the church in the West—has often not realized that the gospel is something that in its very nature you cannot really have and keep to yourself.

Another of the most difficult issues in India today is to discover how the Christian Indian can best influence and actually share in the work of government, whether local, provincial, or national. The new constitution has created a baffling problem by giving the Christian community a communal representation. This imperils the spiritual quality of the Christian church by making membership a political fact that confers a vote. Conversion may thus become a change of political alignment as well as of spiritual allegiance. For these reasons, the majority of Indian Christians were and are bitterly opposed to this communal representation; and their resistance to it was expressed with power by such Indian leaders as K. T. Paul and Dr. S. K. Datta; but without avail.

All too successfuly, also, the West has planted its denominational divisions in Asia. If the church in India can triumphantly overcome these political and separatist evils, the challenge of that achievement to the Christendom of America and Europe will make that church a leader toward world-wide renewal and reunion in a distraught and divided world. To this vital issue we shall return in the last chapter.

III

If the church is to be really rooted in the soil of India one of the first necessities is primary education for the children of the church and their preparation for the Christian life. But when you come to grips with the task on the spot it is almost paralyzing. How is the Christian community in India, with an increase every year now of something like two hundred thousand members, mostly illiterate, to discover and train a staff of teachers with even the barest qualifications? The villages are mostly small. This means that Christians are scattered over wide areas. The parents want the children's earning power to be exercised at the earliest possible moment. Just as soon as they are strong enough to tend goats or scare birds from the crops, they are used for those purposes. The more primitive the background of the child and the simpler the available apparatus, the greater is the demand on the teacher's own initiative. The Christian teacher needs, in addition to an intuitive penetration into the life of his pupils, at once a grasp of his faith and of the subjects he has to teach, and a clear view of the relation of his faith to life and an adequate knowledge of teaching method.

In little mud-and-thatch village schools like one that I visited after bumping over impossible cart-tracks in the Erode district, I saw what was being done, with varying degrees of success, to meet these needs. Small children dressed in a few beads sat on the ground outside the little building learning to write with their fingers in the dust. A group of boys worked out simultaneously sums in arithmetic and problems in nutrition and business from a hanging bunch of bananas in a veranda and a packet of pencils to be bought at one price and sold at another. Seated inside were two older boys, practically young men. These were pupil-teachers learning method from the senior teacher, himself a young man who had been trained at Moga in the Punjab under Dr. and Mrs. Arthur E. Harper and Mr. Sudhir K. Roy, the splendid Indian headmaster there.

The training school at Moga has pioneered in applying the project method to Indian conditions. To describe the project method here would be boring to those who are familiar with its significance and inadequate for others. It is enough to say that all subjects are taught in relation to actual projects, such as the building of a house and courtyard. Arithmetic, including weights and measurements, and geometry with a knowledge of angles and curves, become a natural part of the process of doing the work. Not only is the child the center of the process, but he learns to cooperate with others; not so much to acquire for himself or to outdistance rivals, but to work with them toward a common achievement.

The Bible is at the center of the teaching at Moga and is used with lively and indeed excited interest by the boys and girls for the light that it throws on what they are doing and on the problems they are facing. When I was there a theft had recently taken place in the school. One of the first things the children did was to "comb" the Bible through for light on stealing, and then to discuss, in the light of that teaching, what stealing means to the person who steals, to the person from whom he steals, and to the community in which they both live.

The boys and girls were also studying the world's transport system, beginning with the donkey, the bullock, and the horse to which they were accustomed, and seeing what those animals do in many parts of the world, east and west. They then went on to look at the mechanical transport that replaces and outdistances animals, carrying things and people to and from India. The boys and girls incidentally do very fine expressive art work, both in the actual construction of miniature airplanes, railway trains, and steamships and in making drawings of them.

The degree to which the community of children in the school develops a fresh loyalty within its own frontiers but across other barriers has, I feel, significance for the church itself. One scholar, returning to his village home, had been challenged by his Hindu parents. "You must not," they said, "sit with children of low caste at school. It is wrong." And they went on to name a particular boy. "Why not?" he asked. "He is in my class." In that class were children who were Hindu, Moslem, and Christian—high caste, low caste, and no caste. Is it an overstatement to suggest that in such schools, with their spirit of Christian love, we find the crucible of the new India?

As we have moved from that tiny village school near Erode back to the training institution founded and carried on in Moga by pioneer American Christian educators, and then on into the Hindu village home, we discover one important side of the essential contribution of the Western missionary to the Indian church: the training of village leaders in educational method as well as in the truths of Christ. If we look from the school back to the problem that we considered briefly in an earlier chapter,[1] that of conserving and strengthening the good elements in India's life and of pruning out the others, we find ourselves near to the heart of the answer as we stand before the Christian teacher trained at such centers as Moga. Every habit that the teacher has learned or principle that he has accepted builds up the individual initiative and the equality of opportunity which Indian village life lacks. Yet simultaneously he actually strengthens the spirit and practice of cooperation. The government is showing its recognition of this vital fact by sending men to Moga to be equipped as teachers; it even sends men of exceptional gifts to be trained as governmental trainers of teachers.

The preacher and the teacher, with the poet and musician, can make a nation. In the majority of Indian Christian villages one person is both teacher and pastor; and through them come the songs of the people. As Lascelles

[1] See Chapter Two.

Abercrombie says, "No faith can live that never sings." The training of these teacher-pastors and of their wives is therefore obviously of an importance that words cannot exaggerate. Nowhere is there a clearer call to the West than to contribute the finest educational leadership in this field of equipping the Indian Christian community with the creative leadership that shapes the minds of the new generation, proclaims to them the Good News that gives meaning to life, and leads them to sing the lyrics of eternal life and love. The West can render no more essential or characteristic service to India than to carry to her the profoundest and truest insights that modern psychology and pedagogy can give.

A notable new example of this kind of service was the carrying into India in 1937 by Dr. Frank G. Laubach of his new principles of teaching both adults and children to read, used so successfully by him in the Philippine Islands. He found on examining the Indian problem at first hand that the actual methods used in the Philippine Islands need drastic overhauling in their Indian setting, and that missionaries in different parts of India had been experimenting on similar lines. He was appalled on reaching India to discover that in many areas not ten per cent of those who can read can grasp what they are reading. He is convinced that the reason for this tragic situation is that they have been taught to read the classical language, not the spoken tongue. In cooperation with experts in India he brought out new sets of lessons based on sounds in nine or ten major Indian languages.

As we go to press a vivid picture comes to us of Dr. Laubach coming into a mission compound at Secunderabad, triumphantly carrying the rough copy of a picture textbook in Telugu. "Let us try it out," he said. Three illiterate women who were in the compound were called and they began to learn under his direction. How their mystified faces began to shine as one word after another was grasped! Within half an hour one of the women could read slowly a few simple sentences without the use of the pictures, and she began to teach the others. In the Telugu alphabet there are over four hundred letters, which have been reduced to about ninety in this revised script. An adult who has learned one page must teach that page to a second adult before he learns a second page. So knowledge spreads. A new enthusiasm is growing in adults to learn to read. They will come at eight o'clock in the evening with their little books. Traveling evangelist-teachers are spreading this wonderful development, which at long last makes possible a peasant church that knows its Bible.

The radio-active influence of the power to read the Bible is illustrated in the experience of a woman missionary, who when touring in an area into which no missionaries had, to her knowledge, previously entered, began talking to a group of people in one village about Jesus. To her surprise, instead of being met by the puzzled lack of comprehension natural to such a group on first hearing the gospel story, she was greeted with exclamations and head-shakings indicating agreement. On being asked whether they had heard of Jesus before, they declared that they knew all about him. "Who has told you?" she asked. "Naramma tells us," they replied. On seeking out Naramma, the woman missionary found with astonishment and delight that she was one of her own former pupils who had married into this village. She had been lost to sight by the missionary; but, with the New Testament available in her own language, she had constantly interested the village women with the stories that Jesus told in the parables and with the narrative of his own life, and so had penetrated the community with the leaven of the kingdom of God.

Results, we are told, are accruing from this new method of teaching that seem like magic. The importance of such a development is illustrated by the statistics of literacy and by a comparison of Christian and non-Christian literacy. Of the total population of India, excluding Europeans and Anglo-Indians, only eight per cent are literate,[1] which means that one-third of the world's illiterates live in India. Among the "exterior castes" or depressed classes less than two per cent are literate. Compared with these figures are twenty-two per cent of literates in the Indian Chris-

[1] At the 1931 census there was found to be an increase of literacy in most provinces over the figures for 1921, e.g., 46.9 per cent in the Punjab. In 1931 over five and a half million more Indians were literate than in 1921, an increase of 24.4 per cent, but the increased population figure reduces the proportion of literates to 8 per cent.

tian community. These figures illustrate two outstanding points. First, the remarkably high proportion of literates within the Christian fold compared with those without it, although, owing to the inrush of outcaste Christians, the literacy of Christians exclusive of Burma declined by six per cent during the ten years before the last census in 1931.[1] The second point is that even then the standard of literacy is tragically low. In the long run the only church that is certain of survival as a living force is a church that can read the Bible for itself and understand the narratives that enshrine the revelation of God in Christ. Objection has been raised recently to the mass movements as responsible for lowering the literacy of the Christian church; the argument, however, is not for slowing down evangelism but for increasing efforts for literacy in the church.

IV

In this sphere of the rooting of the Christian community in the soil of India, the buildings in which she worships must play an increasing part. A strongly nationalist Hindu, an expert printer trained in England and

[1] This figure is taken from page 25 of the *Directory of Christian Missions and Churches in India, Burma and Ceylon, 1934-1935*. Comparable statistics are not easy to obtain, and opinions differ on the interpretation of the figures. The Bishop of Dornakal believes that the decrease of literacy among Indian Christians has not been so great as the statement in the text would indicate.

now running an electric printing works in India, spoke to a leading Indian Christian of his certainty that the problems of India cannot be solved until she becomes Christian. When asked why he himself does not become a Christian, he replied that the alien architecture of Christian churches in India and the marks of foreignness in the translations of the Bible make it impossible for him to share in Christian worship.

The adaptation of architecture to the Indian spirit is full of the most intriguing dilemmas. One of them came home to me as I sat at dawn watching the silhouette of the wonderful Christian *ashram* at Tirupatur.[1] At the two ends of this noble house of worship rise great towers modeled on those of a Dravidian Hindu temple, but with, of course, Christian symbols in the tiny sculptures which cover the tower in the Hindu style. I found it as beautiful as it was evidently costly. I discussed it with an outstanding Indian Christian saint, a comparatively young man who is himself the central *guru* in another *ashram* farther south. He is rather markedly critical in temper.

"What impression does this building make upon you?" I asked. "I confess," he replied, "that it shocks me. The reason is," he went on, "that it is modeled much too closely on structures that stand not simply for worship but for Hinduism. They recall the dark evils in the religion on which, as a Christian, I want to turn my back."

[1] Three pictures of this *ashram* will be found on pp. 62, 63, and 65 of *Heritage of Beauty*, by Daniel J. Fleming.

My own conviction is that many Indian Christians would not share this criticism.

The nearest approach to the ideal that I have discovered in India is along the lines of experiment that we see in the cathedral at Dornakal and in the chapel of Trinity College,[1] Kandy. In both cases the hexagonal Dravidian pillar is used, but not the Dravidian temple towers. The carved decoration contains the Cross, the lotus flower as symbol of purity, and the banana as symbol of eternity. At Dornakal the flower of belladonna is also woven into the carving, the deadly poison symbolizing the death that is conquered by eternal life in Christ.

In another sphere I found that a similar sense of repulsion sometimes operates on converts from Hinduism when, as occasionally happens, a group singing Christian lyrics use drums for their accompaniment. Christian converts have told me how the roll of those drums torments them with a deep emotional appeal because all through their boyhood the drums called them to the leaping and dancing festival of the worship of a Hindu god. Christian Indians have also said to me that when the Westerner, seeking to keep to Eastern modes, tries to make his congregation sit on the floor, he is treating as vital an attitude that is quite irrelevant. On the other side, the Victorian Gothic monstrosities that one sees in parts of India, furnished with hideous and unnecessary glass that makes them like demented hothouses, obviously lead the Chris-

[1] See *Heritage of Beauty*, p. 81, for a picture of this chapel.

tian nowhere. The provision of beautiful buildings that will be a fitting environment for the Indian soul seeking God offers a fascinating field for endless inventive and imaginative experiment. An architecture that lifts the soul by its sheer beauty and that is, at one and the same time, Indian without being distinctively Hindu or Moslem, and Christian without being Western, is steadily being wrought out. Will it not rise, in the long run, as our immortal Gothic churches and cathedrals have grown, out of the corporate worship of millions of Christians expressing itself through the chisels and hammers of unnumbered devoted craftsmen?

V

In neither Hinduism nor Islam is there a full equivalent of the Christian pastor. This sets a new problem for the Christian church in India. The conception of the shepherd of souls is one of the profoundly original creations of Christ. Hinduism has its Brahman priest; it has its prophet and saint in the *sadhu*; its teacher in the guru. The functions of a *guru* coincide with one element in pastoral responsibility; the same is true of the prophetic side of the *sadhu's* function. Hinduism, however, has no pastor whose concern is with the day-to-day problems of his flock both as individuals and as a community, and the building up of their mind and character in the faith. Indian Christian pastors worthy and able to handle the "rod and staff" of the Good Shepherd are a vital necessity for the defense and discipline, the guidance and comfort of the Indian church. Moral integrity and solid goodness of heart are the product of contagious Christian companionship sustained through the years.

In addition to this moral task there is an insistent intellectual demand upon the Indian pastor. The voice of Dr. S. K. Datta, principal of Forman Christian College, Lahore, still rings in my ears with his insistence that, unless the Indian Christian pastor grasps intellectually the ultimate meaning of the Cross and the Resurrection, the church will be shipwrecked on the rock of Vedantic philosophy. Hinduism, harking back to that philosophy of "the oneness of all life" from which it springs, is at odds with that tragic mysterious conflict of good and evil which runs right down into the very roots of being. In Christianity we see that conflict dramatized, so to speak, at the historic moment when the forces of evil smote against the love of God in Christ on the Cross. "And ultimately," as the Christian *sadhu*, Matthai, insisted, in talking over these things with me, "it is the living Christ who will sustain the living church. Hinduism can take the historic Christ and incorporate him into its pantheon. It is not even ultimately Christ on the Cross but the risen Christ who will resist those forces of Hinduism that have absorbed into its own structure faith after faith. Jesus in all his earthly life and death may be conceived by Hinduism as one more Avatar of the Eternal; but the divine Christ in his church is not an event in past history, but is the supreme contemporary fact in the daily experience of millions, living in every nation under heaven."

The church in India is indeed a community desperately ignorant, marred with dark blemishes, divided within itself, stumbling at times into the slough of despond from which it is being lifted by its divine Lord. I do not understand, however, how anyone who has seen that church at its worship, met in comradeship the rank and file of its leaders, come face to face with the harsh, loathsome forces that it has to fight, and been lifted in soul by its singing courage, can doubt that, sharing as it does with the holy church throughout the world the grace of its living Lord, it is destined to be the saving salt of India, and from India so to let its light shine that all men may glorify God.

Chapter Five

THE CHURCH AND ITS ENVIRONMENT

I

WHEN YOU WALK THROUGH THE NARROW LANES OF MANY Indian villages, and note with distress the eyes listless with malaria, the limbs gaunt from inadequate food, and the babies a prey to swarms of flies; when you know that the shackles of debt to the money-lender numb the peasant's initiative; when you watch the parasitic cow, the predatory monkey, and the other beasts robbing him of his grain, fruit, and vegetables; and when you see a little band of primitive Christians menaced by these giant evils, your pity for their plight is in peril of sagging into sheer hopelessness. The vitriolic condemnation that Ezekiel pours on the shepherd is terribly true of those high-caste landlords and money-lenders of India who exploit the villager. To no people on earth do these words of indignant sympathy more movingly apply than to the Indian peasant:

> Woe be to the shepherds that do feed themselves! Should not the shepherds feed the flocks? Ye eat the fat, and ye clothe you with the wool, ye kill them that are fed: but ye feed not the flock. The diseased have ye not strengthened, neither have ye healed that which was sick,

neither have ye bound up that which was broken, neither have ye brought again that which was driven away, neither have ye sought that which was lost; but with force and with cruelty have ye ruled them. . . . Thus saith the Lord God; Behold, I am against the shepherds; and I will . . . cause them to cease from feeding the flock; neither shall the shepherds feed themselves any more.

The British rule in India, and the Indian rulers in the princely states and in the new provincial legislatures, can only escape that same condemnation by active creative reform, agrarian and economic.

The peasant, robbed and beaten, lies wounded on the Indian roadside; the priest and Levite have passed him by on the other side. No one who has given allegiance to Him who incarnates the Good Samaritan and the Good Shepherd can divorce himself of responsibility not only for the spiritual new life of rural India but for the peasant's physical health, economic sustenance, intellectual nourishment and social well-being. The Jesus who laid his hand on the leper to heal him and who broke bread to feed the hungry peasants of Galilee, who enjoyed village community life whether as a guest at the wedding feast, or sharing the simple fare of the village home at Bethany, has upon his heart the health, the feeding and radiant living of the disease- and fear-ridden villagers of India. He came that they might have life and have it abundantly.

The writer comes back from India with deep reverence, already expressed in this book, for the heroic work being carried on against fearful odds by the Harijan Sevak Sangh, the Servants of the Untouchables Society, founded by Mr. Gandhi in 1932 and now working in many parts of India. It works for health and temperance, and fights the opium trade; it makes wells for the use of untouchables and fights for their admission with caste people to wells, temples, schools, and roads. The men who are doing this work are in many cases liberal high-caste Hindus. I am entirely convinced, however, that the springs of initiative and of sustained labor to fight these evils and to open the gates of new life cannot be found within Hinduism as a religion. The Brahman cannot, in any case, live among the Harijans. Hinduism, in spite of modern adaptations, is essentially a religion of escape from the suffering that is tied up with the illusion that our personal material life here is real. Hinduism always has been extremely vague and ambiguous on its frontiers, while enshrining a subtle and profound philosophy at its heart and exercising a powerful influence over the hearts of men. At the heart of Hinduism, however, the doctrine of *karma* has produced an attitude of acceptance tinged with despair by chaining men to the irreparable past, while the belief that all is *maya*, or illusion, "weakens," as Dr. Nicol Macnicol says, "the nerve of moral ardor. Life appears meaningless and vain. Its springs are poisoned."

Christ's life and teaching and his whole revelation of reality stand for the opposite view. He shows that our personal being is the offspring of the Creative Person who is

God. There is the core of reality. Responsible relationship, both between men and men, and between men and God, gives life its meaning. Radiant physical health and equality of opportunity for self-expression and service are goals of God's purpose. God is himself the bulwark of freedom and fellowship among his children. If that is the true meaning of life, it never can be reconciled with caste, *karma*, and *maya*. And if caste, *karma*, and *maya* are thrown out, what remains is not Hinduism.

When Indian peasants become Christian in the true sense the new springs of social, hygienic, and economic improvement well up from within them. Something transforming happens when an individual or a group of persons turn from either the terrified propitiation of a goddess-demon of disease or the worship of even a cheerful deity of vital force and "good luck" like the elephant-headed Ganesh, to make a daily approach to "Our Father," asking him to "give us this day our daily bread." They find some distaste for dirt and disorder. They feel the first glimmering of dignity, of the will to freedom, of the power to stand erect.

A tiny window will sometimes open upon a wide and significant landscape. In a village that had just come into the Christian church, the Indian priest had received them all, family by family, and had made up the register. The hundreds of peasants were seated on the ground around him. Suddenly a woman near the front cleared her throat and spat noisily upon the ground, in the customary way.

Her husband, seated behind her, gave her a resounding slap on the back. "Don't you know," he admonished her, "that we don't do those things now we are Christians?"

"We don't do those things now." That is what really happens to the outcaste when he becomes a Christian. "We don't have the neglected gardens, the dirty houses, the heaps of garbage, the messy ragged clothes, the filthy limbs, the disgusting habits. We don't do those things now."

Another window opens on another view of the same panorama of redemption. A depressed-class man who had become a Christian was hailed by his Brahman landlord as he was going to church in long white *dhoti*, his body clean and his hair brushed and oiled.

"You should not wear a coat," cried the rich Hindu, "and you know we say of a Mahar, 'Hit him on the thigh and a cloud of dust rises' "—meaning that he was expected to go dirty.

"Ah," replied the man with a merry smile, "but that is all changed. I am a Christian now."

Are these two pictures crude? We are really face to face with a simple truth of unfathomable significance. Here is something that lies at the very root of a new way of life.

An Indian Christian leader recently expressed to Mr. Gandhi realistically the root of the matter, when the latter had been speaking of the despondency he felt (and that all must often share with him) at the lack of response to the movement to uplift the outcaste. The Indian Christian replied: "I have something transforming to give to the outcaste that you cannot give him in Hinduism, when I say to him: 'The eternal God so loves you that he gave himself for you in his Son, Jesus Christ, so that you may be saved.' An ex-outcaste who believes that God is his Father and loves him like that cannot be crushed. A living spring of new life wells up within him."

II

Is this spirit showing itself in practice within the Christian community in India? Normally the actual guidance of the peasant toward betterment comes through a village teacher-pastor who has had some technical agricultural training, however simple. This Christian village leader at his best knows, for example, where and how the villager can secure better seed, a finer breed of fowl that are more disease-resistant and lay more and bigger eggs. He has access to means for bettering the breed of goats or cows. He knows of a Christian cooperative bank that can eliminate the money-lender by the cheaper purchase of better seed and implements, and by the secure deposit of savings.

An outstanding need, therefore, of the Christian movement in India today is the training of a much more numerous leadership that combines Christian experience, knowledge, and faith with sufficient medical and agricultural technique. The village teacher-pastor-agriculturist can help the peasant with his crops and animals, and in fighting epidemics with antiseptics and with cleanliness. The pastor's wife, similarly trained, can help the women in the village in those aspects of elementary domestic hygiene, such as keeping milk protected from flies, that spell all the difference between life and death, between anemic lethargy and radiant health for the new generation.

The power of the church in India to become self-supporting, also, is rooted in these economic realities. Here is a source of the salaries of the pastors. These economic improvements in India can build up momentous spiritual results. How can the church be self-supporting unless its peasants are better off? This is entirely as it should be in a faith that rests on incarnation and on the redemption of the physical life to spiritual ends.

In order to uplift the villager, the worker must live the life of the village. That great Indian, the late Mr. K. T. Paul, laid down this principle as elementary. This lends high importance to such training as is done, for instance, in places as remote from each other as the agricultural centers directed for a quarter of a century by Dr. Sam Higginbottom[1] near Allahabad, and by the Young Men's Christian Association at Martandam in Travancore, where in the past decade over a thousand pupils drawn from all over India have received training for village leadership. Anyone who, under the enthusiastic guidance of one of the young

[1] Dr. Higginbottom was given by Princeton University the honorary degree of Doctor of Philanthropy, a degree invented expressly for him.

Indian leaders trained at Martandam by Dr. D. Spencer Hatch, has seen the bigger and better goats, sheep and hens, and has watched the process of cooperative collection and marketing of goods, realizes how American hygienic and agricultural training can serve the Christian doctrine of the fullness of life.

Dealing with human garbage is essential. Untold disease, whether by internal poisoning or by hookworm, is due to the absence of the simplest type of latrine. Christian teacher-pastors are spreading the knowledge and practice of simple methods of the cleanly disposal of filth and of its ultimate use in manuring the fields. It is deeply moving and also humorous to hear a great warrior of the kingdom of God like Dr. Higginbottom pass directly from an exposition of Christ's service of health to a lyrical advocacy of the bore-hole latrine.

He is right. The difference between a limp, nerveless, undernourished, spiritless church and one that is vigorous, full of initiative, and able to support a ministry with real leadership lies in such questions. "Cleanliness," said John Wesley, "comes next to godliness." It is certainly the handmaid of the church in India.

Christian hospitals help the health of the rural population; for they increasingly develop simple village dispensaries, reinforced by traveling nurses who carry simple medicines and who see that serious cases are transported to the hospital. Dr. Ida Scudder has, for example, organized a fine roadside traveling service from the well known hospital at Vellore. My own eyes were opened to the help that can be given by simple Indian women with no elaborate equipment when we picked up in our car an old village grandfather with a grandson suffering terribly from ear infection, and landed them safe in the hands of an efficient Christian Indian nurse in her whitewashed hut, with its rows of bottles. These nurses serve their community, however, only when they combine real devotion with adequate technical skill.

The teacher-pastor and his wife go to the hospital in some districts for a fortnight's intensive training by the doctor in the use of some fifteen to twenty simple medicines and antiseptics and the treatment of minor wounds and burns. They then carry back with them to their village a box containing medicines and bandages. Serious cases they pass on either to the Christian or to the government hospital. These teacher-pastors and their wives thus trained prevent and cure much disease, give relief to the suffering of mothers, and win reverence for the Christian ministry. Scattered over the length and breadth of India are tens of thousands of these teacher-pastors. If such simple training were given to all of them, the health of India in its villages would receive greater aid than is achieved by all the government health services.

Some villages, for example, were recently panic-stricken by the dreaded scourge of cholera. Sacrifices were heaped up by the Hindus before the cholera goddess, but with no effect. The Hindu villagers were staggered to find that not one of the Christian community in that area had cholera. What was the cause of this miracle? The pastor-teacher had received just such a simple hospital course as I have described above. He had a bottle of chlorogen. Every jar of water in every home in the Christian community had a few drops of that potent anti-cholera disinfectant put into it before it touched anyone's lips. Then the government officer came to inoculate; the peasants at first refused. The pastor-teacher, however, with the authority that his hospital training gave him, explained the treatment to the Christian community. They then readily came forward for inoculation; and the Hindu caste community followed suit.

This blend of technique with devotion brings us to the root of the problem of the church in India in its relation to its environment. The Royal Commission on Agriculture presided over by Lord Linlithgow (now Viceroy) declared in 1928 the chief hindrance to advance in peasant India to be "the inhibition of the will to progress among the rural population." The central need then is, first, some inner resource producing the resilient initiative that ever works toward a better life. Experiments toward detailed improvement in the daily things of the peasant's life come next. The stubborn resistance to improvement can only thus be overcome. That conservatism is largely due to the tough fabric of Hindu Brahmanical tradition. The Brahman in the Hindu village is the fount of spiritual and moral knowledge. He rivets on the peasants the authority of age-long social custom. He menaces them with the fear of the anger of the gods if custom is departed from. In the long run, the real sustained constructive rural advance will probably take place mainly among Christian peasant communities where there is a sufficient staff of trained teacher-pastors to keep a lamp of knowledge burning steadily and to encourage them to take steps along fresh paths.

Readiness to move forward, however, is ineffective until experiments point a way, and unless some technical skill, however simple, is acquired. A new cockerel is brought into the village. His granddaughters lay three times as many eggs as did their grandmother, and of almost twice the size. When the news of this event spreads from village to village economic progress begins. A better process of weaving with a tougher thread will make a difference to a whole group of villages. In the area, already mentioned, served by the Y.M.C.A. Rural Reconstruction work at Martandam under Dr. Hatch, two hundred families increased the income of each family from twelve rupees a year to one hundred rupees a year by the production of honey. Dr. Higginbottom shows us cows producing more than three gallons of milk to every gallon produced by their grandmothers, and sheep whose wool will fetch many times the financial reward of the shorter, coarser wool of previous generations. On top of this comes help toward the cheaper and better cooperative marketing of the eggs, the honey, and the wool for woven fabrics; and behind the cooperative marketing lie the still barely explored possibilities of cooperative banks.

The peasant church in India can, along these lines, conquer its environment instead of being in imminent peril of being conquered by it. This, it may be objected, is in the sphere of economics. We are bound to reply, first of all, that it springs from the Christian principle that we must subdue the material to be the tool of the spiritual. These peasants can achieve the goal of a self-supporting, self-governing church. To achieve self-support is to solve a root problem of the church in India.

The relation of bad economic conditions to the spiritual and moral degradation of the individual peasant has been vigorously stated by Lord Linlithgow from his profound knowledge. "Debt is the curse of the Indian farmer, for it robs him of the full fruits of his labor, saps his initiative, destroys hope and with it ambition, and darkens the whole outlook of his life. In too many cases, he is born in debt, he lives in debt, and when he dies, his debt is shouldered by his sons."[1]

III

We are thus brought back to the close relation between character and the uplift of the peasant. It is a searching problem in personality. I remember talking with a judge

[1] *The Indian Peasant*, by the Marquis of Linlithgow. London, Faber & Faber, 1932.

near Lahore who told me that he had just had to condemn to imprisonment a Hindu who had secured by bribery the treasurership of a rural cooperative bank and had bolted with the entire savings of the peasants. India's all-embracing need is for men and women in whose very fibre the standards of love and justice, truth and the will-to-serve have won their way. If the Christian community makes that gift to India it will contribute a priceless gift. The fact that over 700 per cent more of the teachers in the government schools of India are Christian than would be expected from the percentage of Christians in the population is due to this blend of character with technical efficiency.

Experiences in Travancore illustrate one solution of the problem of good leadership. A group of prophetic young Indian leaders have developed during this century in company with British colleagues the Alwaye Union Christian College. From the start it has stood triumphantly for corporate interdenominational and interracial leadership. Alongside the college a gallant young Englishman named Lester Hooper brought into being the Alwaye Settlement for outcaste boys, which is still run, after Hooper's early death, by a splendid group of young Indian Christian men and their wives.[1]

Among the many unexpected projects emerging from this group of outcaste boys, all of whom are recruited from

[1] See the author's *Tales from India* (New York, Friendship Press, 1938).

the most hopeless background, was a new experiment in cattle-breeding, started by four of them. These boys were giving devoted care to a few cows and to making a livelihood from the sale of their milk. This led them to dare to dream of a dairy farm. The capital for launching on this venture was supplied in loans from the Settlement Cooperative Society, of which the boys are members. This society combines the functions of cooperative banking of savings and cooperative purchase of tools, seed, and stock. In order to learn the scientific aspects of dairying, one of the group of young Indians who guide the development of the Settlement decided to travel more than a thousand miles northward to Dr. Sam Higginbottom's Agricultural Institute, already mentioned. Here he studied not only the feeding of dairy cattle and the use of medicines for them, and the production of clean milk, but also soils, manures, tillage, vegetable growing, propagation and feeding of plants and their functions, the bacteria and fungi that menace them, and the chemistry of agriculture, with the necessary shop work such as carpentry and ironsmith work.

What has been the result? The boys now have cows each of which produces as much milk as ten or twelve of the cows generally found in that region. This becomes a priceless example in a great area of India where there is plenty of pasturage and widespread need for the milk. The news of this seemingly miraculous improvement spreads far and wide. And as the boys of the Settlement complete their education and pass out into different parts of Travancore, they carry to distant villages this new knowledge of how to effect practical agricultural progress. So keeping good cows in the Settlement by these boys not only exercises their initiative, develops their sense of responsibility, and serves the community by the provision of cheap good milk; it is also of untold service to all the parts of southern India to which members of the Settlement and the students of the Alwaye Union Christian College return when they have graduated.

An able Indian member of the staff of this college sums up under four heads the reasons why appalling poverty prevails. He shows why people are idle while good land remains uncultivated. The list is as follows:

1. Ignorance, with lack of initiative, expectation, and hope.
2. Lack of any kind of capital even for fencing or buying tools.
3. Lack of leadership, whether individual or corporate.
4. Lack of any habits of saving.

Such a simple initiative as has been described above, a project rising from determination to meet a clamant need, grappled with under the conscious direction of God as a specific Christian vocation and equipped with the best technique that modern science can provide, is a direct piece of work by the church of Christ for his kingdom. It reflects Christ's neglected teaching that thought and action are one. Here we see act and idea harnessed by the Christian community to the improvement of a bad situation.

If we move northward from Travancore and follow a group of senior boys and girls from Dornakal, we get a vivid picture of the Christian leaven at work in a village and of the effect of such service on the young people themselves. We are watching through the eyes of Mr. K. J. G. Sundaram of that school the actual work done in a specific week.

When the group of young people reached the village, deep mud and stagnant water made it impossible to walk through some of the streets. Villagers were recuperating from cholera and were mourning the death of many from the awful pestilence. Stagnant, evil-smelling ditches and pools seeped into already poisonous wells. Innumerable flies spread the infection, while at sunset myriads of mosquitoes carried their malarial bacteria.

The Indian students, young men and women, had been inoculated against cholera before setting out on the journey to the village. In their satchels they carried stories and songs on health, cleanliness, and temperance. They had rehearsed dramatic presentations of the evils of drink and the great good coming out of education. Vivid and even gruesome charts and diagrams, drawings and posters showed flies carrying disease from dunghill to baby. They carried lantern slides of healthy mothers and bonny babies.

The camp tents were erected outside the village and the gray-bearded *panchayat* was interviewed. The students explained their visit and pleaded for support and help. This being assured, the party marched through the streets of the village, carrying charts and posters, spades over their shoulders and baskets in their hands, singing health songs at the top of their young voices. From five in the morning till ten at night for a week they kept at their task, which was indeed appalling. Concentrating first on the outcaste hamlet, they tackled the dunghills outside each hut door with shovels and spades. It took two days with twenty hands to cart away the filth in the baskets. They showed the villagers simultaneously how the village could be kept clean, and how its ordure, when put into pits, matured to a condition proper for manuring the fields. They discovered wells surrounded by rags, broken pots, and wild bushes. They cleared the surrounding places and fenced round the wells from the seepage, so that they would be free from poison. On the edge of the village were ponds. Stooping down and looking into the water, they could see the larvæ of mosquitoes. Gathering villagers around, the students poured in kerosene oil. With their own eyes the peasants saw the larvæ dying. Meantime, the women students penetrated the courtyards with brooms and baskets and swept away the refuse of months.

Each afternoon the students paraded the village with health pictures, singing their songs and talking with groups about the evils of insanitation; while in the evening they told stories to the village lads, conducted evensong for the Christians, and then, from a centrally located place, entertained some six hundred villagers with a health drama or a magic lantern show. They gave a *kalakshepam*, blending story and song, on the evils of drink.

One road approaching the village had been impassable for months since the rains because mire three feet deep had become a kind of permanent slough of despond thirty feet long and fifteen feet wide. By filling this with the roots of the weeds pulled up from the fields and with hundreds of basketfuls of sand, the road was restored. Several young villagers, men and women, sat watching the students at work for hours without moving a finger. It would be an interesting if baffling task to try to analyze how far this failure in cooperation was due to lassitude caused by malaria and general anemia; how far it sprang from the doctrines of *karma* and *maya*; and how far from ignorance and incomprehension or fear of the powers of the cholera goddess whose fortress was being so vigorously attacked.

Well before the week was over the village folk in the streets and in their fields were discussing the health work and the meaning of the entertainments. A few of the villagers and the Christian young people joined hands with the visitors. An old man was seen cleaning his courtyard from the rubbish that had lain there for months. A well-to-do merchant sent out his servants with baskets of sand to lay on a muddy public path. The village officials, however, were thoroughly unhelpful, hampered perhaps by the caste system and the inertia of the doctrine of *karma*. The group asked one of them if he would lend them some carts. "Any number of them in a few minutes' time," he replied. But the carts never came and the official disappeared on tour. There were more than a hundred carts in the village. One kind farmer lent his cart but it was requisitioned the following morning by an Indian government servant.

How can we summarize the effect upon the villagers and upon the students? The peasants could never forget the invasion of cleansing and new ideas. The students, who had carried through the work with consistent, good-humored, inventive labor, had seen what it costs to put into practice in face of age-old bad custom Christ's teaching of the unity of thought and action in loving service.

Inner transformation is essential for creating the kind of persons who can either initiate or carry through in a sustained way such Indian rural reconstruction. But those who burn with an inner light can work with those who would achieve an external good. The increasing support given to rural renewal by the government, whether of the British or the Indian states, and by the private initiative of men like Dr. Rabindranath Tagore, calls for cooperative advance. The appointment of Lord Linlithgow brought to the viceregal chair a man whose knowledge of rural India is unsurpassed through his chairmanship of the Agricultural Commission. This has given rural reconstruction a vigorous impetus. In the program of the Indian National Congress as led by Mr. Gandhi, Pundit Jawaharlal Nehru, and Subhas Chandra Bose, the swing has been decisively toward drastic agrarian reform, which Nehru said in August, 1937, is to be the central plank of the program of Congress ministers in running their provincial governments. With all these we find a ground of common purpose.

For Christians a deeper impulse moves. The rural evils in India are seen to run clean contrary to the will of God. We realize that Christian revelation in the East as in the West must spell revolution. As Dr. J. H. Oldham has said:

> It is possible to hold that it is not the task of the Christian church to lay down a social program and at the same time to believe that the Christian faith, sincerely held and acted on, must have a far-reaching, transforming, and, in some directions, a disturbing influence on the whole of social and political life. If it were otherwise it would hardly deserve men's attention.

IV

Imagine a day when the peasants of India will have healthy productive cows and goats and their lands will bear even fourfold the present crops; when the villages will be clean, the houses roomier and more airy, and the children healthier and better fed. Will our goal then be reached? We can well believe that those improvements in physical well-being are agreeable to the will of God and yet be quite clear that even when they are accomplished we shall still be standing on the mere threshold of creating a community on the pattern that represents his purposes. What, we may ask, are some of the changes in the way of living that are called for?

The Indian peasant as he starts on the Christian way begins to learn to build up a Christian home life. This involves drastic changes of relationship between husband and wife, parent and child. The Christian community in the Western world, after a thousand years, is only now moving toward the realization of what Christ's teaching means for the life of woman and for the relationships between men and women. India today is, like the greater part of the human race, so deeply imbued with the doctrine that woman is inferior that only by a miracle of grace can the newly converted Christian husband really grasp Christ's teaching on the subject and put it into practice in his relations with his wife. Equally difficult is it for the girl or the woman to adjust her life to freedom and comradeship. At a dinner in Lahore, in conversation with a brilliant young Indian woman sprung from liberal Moslem stock, I asked her to tell me, in one short sentence, what, to her mind, was the ideal goal for Indian girls. She wrote on a small card, "The Indian girl wishes to blend the dignity and grace of the East with the freedom and adventure of the West." It is a splendid goal—for a Western as much as for an Eastern girl.

A growing class of unmarried Christian women is beginning to grow up even in village India, although a great deal of the work normally undertaken by the unmarried woman in the West is done in India by widows, whose tragic lot is lightened when they come within the Christian church. The movement toward comradeship between young men and women, which is so close to the heart of the growth of a Christian community, is gathering speed and momentum. In 1937, for instance, in the annual interdenominational campaign among villages in the Tamil area of India, twenty girls worked alongside some thirty young men in the singing, the drama, the speaking and the social work. This, we are told, would have been unthinkable five years earlier.

The church feels responsibility for giving guidance to the new generation. The National Christian Council has set up a sub-committee to deal with Christian marriage, divorce, social hygiene, and sex instruction for the young. Frank able pamphlets for girls and young wives are being published.

In the relationships of parent and child subtle differences emerge when parents come within the influence of Christ's attitude toward childhood. For the first five or six years of his life the Indian boy is often the spoiled idol of the home. Directly he is sturdy enough in body to have an economic value he is set to work. With stones and shrill cries he scares birds from the crops. He watches the buffalo and the goat grazing. He runs the errands of the village. He pulls the string that blows the bellows for his father the ironsmith, or helps his father the weaver or potter. It is no lack of love that dictates this exploitation of the years of childhood, but sheer poverty and ignorance.

The boy in the standards of value of Asia as a whole is not regarded as a person in his own right but as a potential adult.

The same is true of the little girl. At an early age she is helping her mother; gathering sticks for firewood, rolling spices, minding the smaller children. The older women know no reticence in front of her; indeed, almost as soon as the little girl can run about she begins to gather knowledge which tends to have a warping and sinister effect on her immature mind. The moment she is fourteen (or earlier in defiance of the Sarda Act[1]) she may be made to go through a marriage ceremony, and by the age of fifteen she may find herself a child-mother.

The village Christian, learning the mind of Christ about the sacredness of childhood, has to be helped and encouraged to make sacrifices to send his children to school, and to defy custom and tradition by refraining from early marriage for them. He and his wife have to be taught to pray with their children and to pass on to them through word and deed their own new-found faith. Only so can the children grow up with a real experience of Christ and a habit of relating their conduct to the will and purposes of God.

Indeed, the redemption of the Christian's social life,

[1] Miss Margaret Read writes in *The Land and Life of India*, "The Sarda Act of 1931 fixed the age of marriage for boys at sixteen and for girls at fourteen, but the consensus of opinion is that in circles where early marriage is the custom, the Act is not being observed."

whether rural or urban, opens up a great work for the church. Clough's lines about the converts

> Who cry "O easy yoke of Christ"
> But find 'tis hard to get it on

are poignantly true of the Indian Christian living in a Hindu or a Moslem setting. When the first glow of his conversion begins to fade, the Christian may hanker wistfully after the light and excitement of the religious festivals, the bouts of toddy-drinking, the excesses at weddings and at funerals. Tragic results come when the Christian life is penned in by a quickset hedge of galling prohibitions.

By means of song and drama as well as the making of cleaner, more beautiful homes and gardens, the Christian church is in many areas triumphantly creating a widening horizon of free self-expression, but this work of priceless value must be multiplied a hundredfold. Adventure is called for in the inventive creation of a lively Christian pattern of life, full of action and color. For the Hindu, Moslem, or animist, religion creates the framework of his life; it dictates his every action, almost his every thought. When he becomes a Christian he is in peril of losing this framework without really gaining another that is truly Indian. He needs to feel himself a member of a divine fellowship stronger and more far-reaching, more warm-blooded and more filled with active meaning than the one he has left. This comradeship must care for the material and social needs and cravings of all ages and both sexes, as well as for their religious nourishment. To achieve this and to rise victorious over the barriers of caste and class, sex and nation, the church, as in the first century, must be the convert's social and economic as well as his spiritual home —a place where Christians have all things in common.

The word "reconstruction" was deliberately used by that great Indian Christian nationalist, K. T. Paul, when he coined the now universal slogan "rural reconstruction." He held that the goal in view is not the creation of rural India on new lines, but the reshaping of village life on lines loyal to the ancient pattern of mutual aid, yet freed from the evils that are now breaking that pattern. So the watchword is not "construction" but "reconstruction." It is significant that even the project of an India-wide government commission on agriculture should have sprung originally from the mind of this man who is at once profoundly Indian and profoundly Christian.

The model plan, similarly, on which progress is now envisaged both in government and in Christian circles was developed out of world-wide experience by an American Christian leader, the late Dr. Kenyon L. Butterfield. His plan, which is now being adopted and adapted in China, Japan, and Africa, sees a group of villages as a unit—a community, to be served by a trained pastor-teacher-agriculturist and his wife. The goal is the development of a rural Christian church that shall feel every part of the life of that group of villages to be its concern. This plan is the most effective yet devised for solving the problem of how to make each rural community an integral yet individual fragment of the world community of the kingdom of God. Their knowledge of the care of babies and of chickens and calves, their purchase of seed and the handling of village sanitation are as integral to the Christian service of the community as are the development of Christian song and prayer and Bible reading, and the proclaiming in church and village street of the word of God.

We are face to face with a new program for the missionary as well as for the Indian if we see the service of Christ in India as including, first, leading the peasant craftsman and farmer to decisive and intelligent Christian discipleship; and, second, teaching them to make the best use of the soil, of the plants and animals dependent upon it, and the minerals within it. The soil is the gift of the Father. The use of the earth is our stewardship of his gift. The Christian farmer working more efficiently serves the greater glory of God. The feeding of the future generations of India depends on the peasant. So does the sustenance of the church of Christ, the salaries of its pastor-teachers, and the virility and happiness of its rank and file. By embracing with wholehearted, intelligent, and inventive planning such a program of advance the Christian folk of the furrow can participate in the major goal of the Indian people, which is rural peace and prosperity achieved through a coherent Christian pattern of community life.

Christian teachers and preachers must work together to create a rural civilization Christian to the core. That is the most secure foundation on which to build a new India. Each little Christian group of villages is only a tiny fragment of the kingdom of God in India. Can we, however, see a limit to the power of these multitudes when Christianized and mobilized for national harmony and for international peace?

Chapter Six

LEADERSHIP FOR THE NEW INDIA

I

SITTING IN THE DRAWING-ROOM OF THE PRINCIPAL OF A GREAT college in India in a circle of Indian students, I could not help wondering from what homes and from what background they had emerged. To me the most startling result of questioning the group on this point was to discover how many of them had actually come from village homes, whether Moslem, Hindu, or Christian. I repeated this inquiry in similar circumstances in different parts of India. As we watch the Indian student and try to look through his eyes at life, with the adventure that it offers and the demands that it makes, it is essential to remember that we are to a considerable degree dealing with someone who is in the majority of cases a product of the village and may himself ultimately go back to sow in the village the seeds of change.

As I thought of this group of students, both as men in need of the Good News of Jesus Christ, and as potential leaders in the church in India and the world, the question to which I sought an answer was, "What are the forces beating in upon these young men and women, as they come out from the background of Moslem or Hindu homes into the new secular college or university world?"

We see a senior adolescent Hindu boy, with his small tin trunk and his roll strapped in a gaily colored rug, stepping out from the courtyard of his village home to take the bus to the train which will carry him to the great city. All through his younger boyhood the immediate surroundings of this Brahman boy have been the larger family and especially its women folk. His father's mother has been the ruler of the household. An atmosphere of loving kindness has been round him. As a boy, his own mother and the wives of his uncles have conspired to spoil him. In the background he has seen the widows of the family, pathetic in their resignation to an empty and purposeless loneliness. He has performed his devotions in the little domestic prayer-room. He has drawn in from the very atmosphere the sense of capricious spiritual forces. Magic and everything that contradicts the sense of scientific law is the ever present setting of this uncertain life. He has heard the discussions of how his sister and girl cousins are to be married. If his father is a true Brahman he has also in his early teens received insights into Vedantic philosophy and spiritual reality.

Thus the immemorial ways of Indian life, the standards of value that have prevailed across Asia, seep into his consciousness and determine his emotional reactions and daily decisions. Then one morning he starts out to the government or missionary high school in the nearest town.

On the athletic field, in the dormitory, and under his teacher's eye in the schoolroom he begins to make choices for himself, to be driven to take personal initiative, to get a glimmering of scientific law, and a perspective, however vague, of the great world. These foreshadowings of Western education contradict many of his early habits of mind and traditional attitudes.

From high school he takes the far more revolutionary leap to college. The train runs through the sprawling suburbs, and at last he alights and comes out into the busy streets of Calcutta or Madras, Bombay or Lahore, where every sight or sound still further challenges the old values. Sports like tennis, cricket, and football brace him and bring him under the discipline of the critical judgment of young men of his own age. Professors in their lectures open up vistas of fresh facts and ideas. While some of his teachers simply grind out the modicum of knowledge needed to pass an examination, he finds one or two whose living vision of reality and whose forward-looking minds stir his imagination. Most Indian students face education as a process whose reward is lucrative service that may make life easier for their parents. Here and there a sense of definite vocation is quickened.

Some older students air their sophisticated derision of the ancient ways. Bookshops offer unexplored ranges of science and history. The youth buys paper-backed vernacular novels that open up vistas in which sentimentalism, crime, and sex are strangely blended. He or his friends have cheap phonographs from which are played in jostling alternation stirringly beautiful Indian lyrics and raucous jazz dance music. On the walls of his friends' rooms are, according to their varied tastes, photographs of Nehru, Gandhi, Tagore, and blonde American movie stars, while the moving pictures intoxicate his senses with the irresistible stimulation of the emotions.

As one term succeeds another at college or university, the youth's allegiance may, in his search for reality, swing from one group to another. Here are young men, dressed in *dhotis* with folds carefully arranged, who drift in and out of each other's rooms, and read aloud to each other the poems that they have written in their own vernacular, be it Bengali or Punjabi, Tamil or Telugu, under the inspiration, say, of the earlier T. S. Eliot or the Sitwells. Or they may exchange short stories written after reading D. H. Lawrence or Aldous Huxley. And while they burn incense to these Western gods, their verse or prose will also emulate that of Rabindranath Tagore or Sir Mohammed Iqbal, the Nietzschean Moslem poet of the Punjab. Proscribed books by nationalist rebels are eagerly passed from hand to hand. He finds on the shelves of the young professors in the university the books that were the inspiration of the heyday of Gandhi's influence—Tolstoi, Dostoievski, and Romain Rolland. The student himself, however, when he swings from the group of young literary intellectuals to the social revolutionaries, reads Harold Laski, whose influence is widespread throughout India, and Jawaharlal

Nehru's autobiography. Karl Marx himself is, for most students, too rigorous an intellectual diet when so many predigested summaries of his thought are at hand. In the occasional solitude of his own cubicle, the student feels the thirst for the Eternal Spirit in whose existence pseudo-science and materialistic economics have shaken his belief. A superficial modernism has eaten like acid into his primitive belief, but has set no new vision in its place.

Led perhaps by the rumor that Mr. Gandhi reads the Bhagavad-Gita every day, he may open its pages and read:

"He who rejoices not, hates not, grieves not, desires not, who renounces alike fair and foul, and has devotion is dear to me."

The twentieth-century Indian student, however, finds, on the contrary, that he himself is grieving and desiring, that he is very ready to rejoice and then to hate; and is most reluctant to renounce. "Am I," he asks himself, "to affirm life and grasp it with both hands; or am I to deny it, and escape its joys and torments?"

Caught in these suffocating uncertainties of youth he may be led by some friend to one of the modern expressions of reformed Hinduism. He may visit, for instance, one or other of the Ramakrishna monasteries. There the monks, with shaven heads and saffron robes, alternate between meditation that aims at escape from the thraldom of desire, and active help to orphan boys in a workshed as they learn a craft, or in the dispensary where villagers come for healing. The student is told that the great seer,

Ramakrishna, received revelations from Christ and Allah and Kali; and that through the discipline of this monastery he himself may hope to reach union with the universal Divine Essence. Yet as he reads in his daily paper, such as *The Hindu*, a speech by Nehru calling youth to sweep away from India the imperial tyranny of Britain and the economic despotism of the Indian landlord and capitalist manufacturer, he tingles to the finger-tips. Sri Ramakrishna exhorts him to wait and meditate until he is free from desire and from the call to action. But the voice of Mother India makes him leap to his feet and leave meditation for the path of revolutionary action.

A genuine patriotism and an ideal of social service are now permanent influences in Indian student life. The student needs Western as well as Indian teachers who can reveal in living terms the path of good citizenship. Such teachers must train new men who will not only be the architects of India's future political institutions, but also able to use those institutions for the good of the people.

The student responds to the enchantment of the human pageant. Along the street of an Indian city he sees the merchants behind their bales of cloth and heaped-up sweetmeats, the crippled leper, the whining beggar, the fly-infested babies on the hips of their little sisters, the sacred bull nosing his way into the vegetable market, the taxis honking at the bullock wagons, the coolie with heavy-laden curved basket balanced on his head—and they all lure him away from contemplation of the unconditioned Absolute. The ongoing life of pulsating humanity calls to him to take his share in the drama.

Before coming to college the student has probably been betrothed and possibly even married to an illiterate girl for whom these new experiences that have changed life for him have little meaning. In his college days he may find himself meeting girl students on terms of equal comradeship.

The life of the Indian girl student today tingles with even more adventure than that of her brother, because she comes into the new India from a more secluded background. From the *zenana* to the classroom is a far cry. To travel from the circle made up by her illiterate grandmother, mother, and aunts to the dormitory where eager girls of her own age read Aldous Huxley's *Brave New World* and discuss every aspect of the Duke of Windsor's romance is to leap across chasms that the West has taken centuries to bridge. Never in history have so many women revolutionized life so swiftly as did the thousands who swept out of their homes at the call of Mr. Gandhi in his non-cooperation campaign. These girls and women came from secluded Oriental homes into the rough-and-tumble of street processions. They endured rioting and picketing. They faced the police court and the prison. The changing of social sanctions and the opening of educational opportunity to womanhood are not trivial or passing features but part of a major transformation. To quote only two expert opinions, the Director of Public Instruction of the Moslem state of Hyderabad told me that he did not think that *purdah*—the life behind the curtain—could survive there for more than another ten years; and Professor N. C. Mukerji of Allahabad Christian College exclaims, "The *zenana*, like the Bastille, has fallen." The fact that multitudes of young peasant women have been swept into mills and factories creates another aspect of change.

As the student talks with his comrades in the university about his future, futility and frustration descend upon him. For scores of thousands of young Indians Western education is the avenue through which they join the ever increasing multitude of educated unemployed. As Professor Mukerji says: "For the fathers education was a passport, for the children it is a disadvantage leading nowhere."[1] Mr. Mukerji himself propounds a scheme with the goal not only of lifting youth out of this trough of despair but of leading India to a high new plane of life. He would call the new governments, provincial and central, throughout India, to swing the educated unemployed into the nation-building departments of government.

"We will have," he says, "to break through all records and think in new categories, if we are to be of any help here. It should be possible to organize and finance on an India-wide scale a corps of social servants, men and women who would live on a basis of sharing, and experiment in

[1] *The Revolutionary Mind in India To-day.* Allahabad, 1937.

simpler living. They should not be exploited by being asked to live the ascetic life on the zero scale. On the other hand, a moderate standard of an educated man's life, not very lavish nor very meager, should be ensured them. Adequate medical aid, facilities for proper education of children, protection in old age, should be made available to them. They should further have every chance of keeping up their intellectual life and increasing their experience in every possible way, so that the country would get their very best. Within the bounds of such a service, there will be room enough and to spare for all the educated unemployed. We can thus turn a disaster into an opportunity."[1]

Sir Daniel Hamilton of Bengal has propounded a similar idea. He holds that if rural India were organized on a cooperative basis as is the case on his estate in Gosaba, near Calcutta, the public services—education, health and so on—would absorb a vast number of educated unemployed.

These schemes, however, bring no immediate help to the student today as he faces a world that all too frequently in India, as in the West, has no use for his services. Unemployment has intensified rebellious attitudes. Blame is heaped upon both the government and on the employers of labor. The revolutionary mood of youth, as I met it in all parts of India in 1937, was strong in Christian as well as in Hindu and Moslem groups, but was strongest of all among the young agnostics. The political liberalism

[1] *The Revolutionary Mind in India To-day.* Allahabad, 1937.

that believes in the "inevitability of gradualness" has been swept out of the mind of India's youth by the earthquake of Gandhi's nationalism followed by the rushing wind of Nehru's Marxian socialism. The extreme form of this is expressed in Professor Mukerji's declaration that "youth has bartered God for Lenin and believes in a resurrection through the gateway of revolution." "Youth," he adds, "has given up God. But hero worship still survives and youth is prepared to make the great sacrifice in following the Leader of its choice."

What we are faced with in Indian student life is normally not a logical coherent orthodox type of Marxian socialism. Gandhi and Karl Marx are strange bedfellows; but they share the hospitality of Pundit Jawaharlal Nehru's mind, which, indeed, is still in a process of evolution. Nehru, as he advocates Marxian ideas, gives a long lingering look behind to the principle of soul-force and of *ahimsa*, or harmlessness, yet expresses a reluctant admission that force may need to be used; while, in his socialist thought, the family and private property are not banned.

Many students, while reverencing Gandhi personally, smolder with discontent at what they regard as the futile policy of non-violent non-cooperation which carried their elder brothers by the thousand into prison, and was called off without achieving the goal of home rule. In other moods, however, they see that non-violent non-cooperation is a potent weapon, whether handled as boycott or sheer moral demonstration. Indeed many would hold that it caused the striking victory won by the Congress party at the first elections under the new constitution in 1937.

The student carries back into his village home and environment these discontents and new visions. He talks in rebellious anger not only against the alien government but against the usurious money-lender, the avaricious landlord and his agents. He girds against the static age-old social customs of his Hindu or Moslem background. He sees, however, no coherent alternative picture of human relations, whether in the family, in industry, in the village, in the nation, or internationally.

II

The drastic criticism hurled at education in India is that, through becoming increasingly utilitarian, it is losing its real usefulness. The explanation of this paradox is that education has been planned to prepare men for a modern professional type of career, that of the lawyer and so on; but India's need today is for technicians, men who can really build a new community life in India. India, which is, as we have seen, village India, needs skilled agriculturists—men with a strong sense of community, practical economists of real integrity; leaders who can organize and run cooperative banks and cooperative purchasing and marketing systems. India needs first-class craftsmen and engineers. Experts are wanted in the simplest yet most modern forms of adult education of rural people. Artists, writers, and editors are required who can interpret modern knowledge to simple rural communities. Pioneers are called for to work out ways in which the villages can be led to take full advantage of the riches of broadcasting. Inexhaustible possibilities of enlightenment lie in the traveling moving picture. Great careers lie before men and women who will spend their lives in the spread of preventive hygiene as well as of curative healing.

How can we help toward this great goal? Colleges and universities, and especially the Christian institutions of learning, can win and sustain recognized creative leadership by swinging adventurously into supplying the needs of the rural community. Instead of looking to professional work in the city, young Christian graduates are called to bring to the service of the peasant such missionary enthusiasm as the Mysore government's electric staff throws into carrying light into the peasant's home and power to help him in the irrigation of his fields and the threshing of his crops. To carry "light and power," not electric, but spiritual and moral; this is a work that will test the most highly gifted.

The universities and colleges can supply India's greatest need—skilled devoted social servants—and can simultaneously move those who control the springs of government, whether Indian or British, to organize government service to that end. Today the secular universities—with all their good gifts—do one disservice: they add one more class, and that a large unemployed one, to India's plethora of classes. The real task of the universities is to create the creators of a society organized for the corporate service of the common good.

The need for such service has been pleaded with authoritative eloquence in the Report of the Commission on Christian Higher Education in India. They say:

> The gulf between the educated classes and the ordinary citizen is greater in India today than it ever was in nineteenth-century England. The university education which is intended to fit men for the higher professions and for government service does not fit them to understand the actual needs of the ordinary people whom they have to serve. Rather it removes them into a different world of ideas. So long as that remains true, university studies and university researches will probably be remote from the problems and experience of the people as a whole and academic in the wrong sense of the word. What is perhaps even more serious, so long as this isolation of the universities persists, there can be no active public opinion on education in India, and we have found the absence of such a public opinion one of the great weaknesses in college education.

Democracy will be an illusory ideal in India until there is an educated electorate, until at least there is a leaven in the general population who have the knowledge to administer all those forms of local government and democratic organization which must exist between the people and the government. There are the beginnings of popular movements in India, but unless the leaders which they throw up are equipped with knowledge of the problems they face, they will bring about little but disillusionment.

There is in India today a great mass of knowledge, largely collected by government, which if applied would go far to help the problems of village India. The difficulty is to get it applied. For knowledge can only really help people who have learned to believe in it. The Agricultural Institute at Allahabad, after many years of experimenting, has found a fruitful way of broadcasting its researches through the training of village teachers. That is only one example of a service which the universities of India could render to the nation in countless ways.[1]

Christian colleges are, as we have already seen, showing a growing practical interest in rural reconstruction. They carry out research into actual conditions and into the causes of evils. They lead positive social service. American and British mission boards have responsibility for colleges that are making notable experiments and are in many cases feeling the need to go much further. Among these are the Forman Christian College, Lahore, St. Stephen's College, Delhi, and St. John's, Agra, in the north; St. Paul's, Calcutta, and Serampore College in the east; the Madras Christian College and the Women's Christian College, Madras, and the American College at Madura in the south; and Wilson College, Bombay, on the west, to name only a few that I have had the opportunity of seeing at first hand.

The Reverend Stephen Neill at times carries out with his students of the Diocesan Theological College of the

[1] *The Christian College in India*, p. 372. London, Oxford University Press, 1931.

Tinnevelly district of South India the plan of sending a group of men to live in a Christian village for a week. They visit the people in their houses, make friends, and hold private talks as well as meetings with all sorts and conditions of men. In this college there are students from the Madras, Rangoon, Colombo, and Singapore dioceses, in addition to Tinnevelly, as well as from the Indian community in Natal, South Africa. After a quiet day and conference, followed by the ticklish business of getting over fifty men transported to seven scattered points along the roughest of country tracks, the work begins. From the central station, a market town with a great Hindu temple, Mr. Neill and Father Carleton of the Oxford Mission, as organizers of a recent enterprise on these lines, went out every day to visit one or other of the groups. For those who will take the pains to analyze its significance, we can hardly give a better picture of the group work among one of the largest congregations than that drawn in a letter to his friends by Mr. Neill:

In my preliminary instructions I had written of this: "A desperate congregation; those belonging to this group had better bring crowbars and dynamite." But my gloomy forecast proved entirely wrong; the people most warmly welcomed the campaigners, crowded to the meetings, invited them into their houses, provided a feast for us on the day of our visit, and ordered Bibles and prayer books, at the reduced rate, in almost alarming numbers. I think that this was more than a passing emotion, and that the congregation really has begun to come alive.

The agonizing suffering and the nerveless lassitude that Indian diseases have laid upon the Indian people bring home poignantly the great need for leadership in the ministry of healing. In order to see in perspective the total need the National Christian Council, allied to the Christian Medical Association of India, have a comprehensive plan. They propose a Union Christian Medical College. Anyone who has seen the eager faces of Indian girls being trained at Vellore to minister to the suffering women of India, or at the Lady Hardinge Medical School and hospital at Delhi, or again at Ludhiana, or the men students at Miraj preparing for the parallel task, must hope that, however great may be the financial demands of an adequately equipped Christian medical college, they may be met in the spirit of the Great Physician. An adequate and sustained supply of Christian doctors and nurses of finest quality is a path to leadership open to the best spirits in young India.

The next revolution in education in India must be to use higher education for creating armies of servants of primary education, and thus correct the preposterous top-heaviness of the system. A survey of the results of higher education in India creates the conviction that woman's education has developed far better products in this service for the social good than has that of men. An examination, for instance, of the former students of the Women's Christian College, Madras, gives a heartening sense of the creative India-wide contribution of first-class education rooted in a real faith.

Rich and radiant possibilities lie before the equipped Christian girl students of India today as they face the shaping of the new life of women in the emerging India of tomorrow. The centrality of the work of Christian women to the ongoing life of the church is, of course, as old as the faith. It dates from the days when the mother of James and John, with Mary and others, ministered to the group of disciples around our Lord and to him; and when St. Paul challenged his friends at Philippi to rally to the aid of his women colleagues, Euodia and Syntyche, saying, "Help these women, for they labored with me in the gospel."

No development of women's work among peasants is more salutary and striking than that through which the women evangelists, usually known as Bible-women, are now passing. In the past they have rarely had any real education. Visiting the *zenanas* to explain the Bible to the women of the home, telling the gospel story to patients in hospitals, and in other ways they have done sterling service. But, generally speaking, while often devoted Christians, loyal and loving, who give themselves without stint, they are a dependent, subservient group of semi-literate women with a very elementary acquaintance with the books of the Bible and with the outline of the tenets of their own denomination. Even their primitive equipment, of course, gives them a deeper sense of the meaning of life and a rather larger outlook than that of the secluded, lonely, illiterate women to whom they go. But increasing multitudes of young women from village as well as city are discussing new ideas and entering social and industrial life. Educated young Christian women leaders can do great work in this field. Western missionaries are needed to cooperate with Indians in training this new leadership.

One example of this new trend is to be found in the Girls' Training School at Medak. The basic idea of this school is that the girls in training as Bible-women and teacher-evangelists' wives should have a real course of preparation for their future lives in the villages of India.

They live, therefore, in houses like little village houses. Each student has charge of several children. She lives with them, cooks for them, mends their clothes and "mothers" them as well as teaching them in the model kindergarten during the day. The students, besides studying the Bible, learn modern kindergarten methods, Indian music and how to conduct singing, handicrafts and gardening. When they have finished their course they are not only trained educationists but trained mothers, prepared to embark on their heroic and often lonely task of demonstrating the Christian life in the villages.

The old tradition of economic, mental, and spiritual dependence on Western missions and the adoption of the standards of value of Western leaders is impossible for anyone who would minister effectively to this young newer group. How, we are bound to ask, can India secure an educated woman leadership that is independent in spirit and in status; that enjoys an integrally Asiatic education; that has a grasp of higher truth and yet has not lost the "common touch"? That leadership must be equipped to guide the social, economic, health, educational, and recreation needs of Indian young women and children. These high and difficult but entrancing tasks cannot be performed by any mission or denomination in isolation. A start has been made in replanning curricula, led by the Committee on Religious Training of the National Christian Council. St. Christopher's Teachers' Training College in Madras, which nine American and British missionary organizations combine to support, already has a fine curriculum that relates religion to life.

To lift the service of women in the Christian community in India to so high a level that the ablest and best qualified young women of the nation will be attracted to it may be an arduous task. After all, however, it is less Herculean than the revolution that lifted nursing in Britain from the vile grossness that Dickens caricatured in Sairey Gamp to its present dignity and efficiency. Indian women must take an increasing measure of freedom and self-direction within the planned program of the mission and of the church. The curricula for their training, the staff that teaches them, the standard of efficiency demanded, have to be raised notably. As one example of progress we note that young educated Indian women are beginning to apply themselves to painting or drawing pictures to illustrate religious literature, and to writing lesson outlines.

Christian women are breaking into many varieties of social work in the cities. In the slums they help the factory women and girls; they themselves live in social settlements. In college and university areas they run hostels for students. The Y.W.C.A. offers in some cities an all-round program of education, recreation, and personal spiritual counsel. They are also giving support, in fellowship with women of all faiths, to the fight against opium, which Mr. Gandhi is leading with such vigor. This drug is responsible for the death every year of unnumbered babies in the *chawls* (the workers' tenements). They are fighting against liquor-traffic, prostitution, and the exploitation of child labor. It is not possible to see the limits of the superb pioneering work to be done tomorrow by Christian women of the East and of the West who throw themselves with zest and dedication into the service of girls and women. If we are asked what type of women are ideally needed, the reply would be those who are developing character and mind that blend Eastern fortitude, patience, and insight with Western resource and initiative. They must enjoy working with people rather than for them. They must present a living faith in a form natural to the peasant mind, by deed as well as by word.

This brings us back to the multiplication of men and

women students who will become teacher-pastors and wives of teacher-pastors. These alone can build a new India in the place where India lives and will always live—the village. In the creation of those creators of the new India, the Western missionary will continue, as all Indian Christian leaders say again and again, to play a large rôle. The church in India would be paralyzed if it were Indian without being a conscious part of the church universal, the *una sancta* of which all true Christians are indeed members. The task of helping to create this school of the prophets for rural India will call into play every inborn gift and acquired skill of the missionary; all his physical stamina and spiritual grace. The rural church needs first-class men thoroughly trained, not in abstract things but in the equipment and the spirit needed in the village. Here the demands are fully as subtle and exacting as are those for city work. Balance must be sustained between classroom and field work. This makes the classroom more realistic and the field work more inventive. What man is or could be too brilliant or powerful to find his every resource called into full play by working at close quarters with all sorts and conditions of Indians, Moslem and Hindu, in agricultural fairs and markets, in peasant gospel schools that bring together the leadership of groups of villages, and in translating into Indian parable form by speech and by song those truths that Jesus gave to the peasant farmers and craftsmen of Galilee?

III

There are many Hindus who are confident that Hinduism can itself provide the seed and the growth of a sustained Indian leadership of integrity, vision, moral drive, and technical efficiency. Characteristic of this modern view of some leading Hindu intellectuals are the eloquent words of Sir Sarvapalli Radhakrishnan: "In my travels round the country and abroad," he writes, "I have learned that there are thousands of men and women today who are hungry to hear the good news of the birth of a new order, eager to do and dare, ready to make sacrifices that a new society may be born, men and women who dimly understand that the principles of a true religion, of a just social order, of a great movement of generosity in human relations, domestic and industrial, economic and political, national and international, are to be found in the basic principles of the Hindu religion. Their presence in growing numbers is the pledge for the victory of the powers of light, life, and love over those of darkness, death, and discord."[1]

An eminent Moslem, again, expresses the impatience of the modern reforming spirit with Islamic orthodoxy; Sir Shafaat Ahmad Khan, professor of modern Indian history in the University of Allahabad, says: "The Indian

[1] *The Legacy of India*, edited by G. T. Garratt, p. 286. New York, Oxford University Press, 1937.

young men and women who are starting their life are impatient of the lumber of ages which is sometimes represented as the quintessence of wisdom, and will make short work of those who oppose their path."[1]

This leads to an outstanding and so far entirely unsolved problem in the relation of education to personality. Hundreds of thousands of young Indian students and graduates were brought up as small children, in the years when their emotional pattern of life was shaped, within the traditional Hindu and Moslem ancient ways of life in the *zenana* and the harem. Modern education has during school and college years superimposed on this substratum a cold slab of Western ideas and technical science that contradict the ancient pattern. Their mind is at desperate odds with their emotions. Personality is disintegrated. Internal conflict exacerbates jangled nerves. They hit out rebelliously at the old order, curse the existing government and decry modern secularism as bankrupt. Disillusionment gives birth to wrath and bewilderment.

Life is re-illumined for thousands by hero-worship of Pundit Jawaharlal Nehru. In princely self-giving he surrendered wealth, a promising legal career, and the joys of a brilliant international social circle for prison and the dust and heat of the political arena. This example gives meaning to life to students of every or no religious faith, and in all parts of India. He calls them to a vigorous

[1] *The Indian Federation*, by Sir Shafaat Ahmad Khan, p. 339. New York, The Macmillan Co., 1937.

social and economic transformation. His India-wide political campaign took place while I was traveling to and fro across his tracks. This enabled me repeatedly to test the impression that he created in the cities where he was speaking. I found that his honest, direct, astringent call to hard work, rigorous self-discipline, and sustained fortitude chilled the spirit of many merely emotional youths but stiffened and strengthened the steady determined loyalty of men with more grit.

A second test is in process. Under the new constitution of a United States of India, in 1937 more than forty million voters elected their own assemblies. They placed on the shoulders of the Congress, of which Nehru is president, the responsibility for giving a new and constructive lead for India. The fervor of the political rebel is now harnessed to the tasks of social and economic reform. Congress politicians promised the peasant that they would ease from his bent shoulders the intolerable burden laid there by the landlord, the tax-collector, the money-lender, and the priest. These promises must be made good by legislation followed up by administrative action.

Into this world young educated India is moving. The memory of some talks with young Indian graduates in Madras, Hyderabad, Calcutta, Bombay, and Lahore haunt me. Inconsolable mystics, they cannot breathe in the stifling caves where the old mythologies molder. Yet they refuse to be intoxicated by the new myths of nation, party, or race. Freed from the yoke of dead traditions, they fear to become the slaves of the new mechanism. No doctrine satisfies them; but the absence of convincing insights into truth torments. The cisterns that supplied the spiritual and moral water of life to their fathers are broken; but they can discover no new fountain of living water. The ancient foundations of India seem to sag beneath them. They seek for a new conception of life; but in the search they experience a deep distress. For if they look to the Far West or to the Far East they discover neither in the bewildered inquietude of a disillusioned America, nor in the aggressiveness of a super-industrialized imperialized Japan, a lamp for the feet of an emerging India. If they look to Europe they see unchained demoniac powers hurrying her panic-smitten herds down the Gadarene steep. Such students of India today, who bring to life a desire to grasp its meaning, to grip hold of it, and to conquer its evils, are—like their fellows in the West and in the Far East—a tormented generation.

IV

The contribution that a truly Indian and truly Christian student community can make to the leadership of the church in India deepens the significance of the work of those Western Christians who are bringing the intelligentsia of India face to face with the living Christ. The work of Dr. Stanley Jones in this field has emphasized the principle of sharing truth in what is known as the round table method. Here all share their partial insights into truth, and the light that can be shed by each faith on the meaning of life is expressed by those who have seen that light. This is not syncretism, or the fitting together into a pattern of elements from each faith. Its outcome, seeing that in Christ all truth shines, is to lead men toward him.

Dr. Jones's evangelism combines the logic of the teacher and the fervor of the prophet. His power to draw large audiences of Hindu and Mohammedan as well as agnostic and materialistic students makes his presentation, for instance, of the Marxian and the Christian alternative solutions of contemporary problems of peculiar interest. Speaking in English to students and other educated Indians in all the main centers of university and collegiate life, his message is one that powerfully reinforces the day-to-day work of teaching and preaching carried out year after year by the teachers and professors as well as by the evangelistic missionaries, who bear the burden and heat of the day, often with all too little recognition.

In addition to round table conferences, Dr. Jones has undertaken, in recent years, a new enterprise—the founding of two *ashrams*. The desire to develop on Christian lines the *ashram* ideal in India has led to numerous experiments from Travancore in the far south, by way of Tirupatur in Madras, right up to the foothills of the Himalayas. There Dr. Stanley Jones has initiated a fellowship at Sat Tal near the summer capital of the United Provinces.

The essential factor in creating an *ashram* is a guru or teacher, who lives in a place with his disciples gathered round him for longer or shorter periods to absorb his spirit and his teaching. Two mottoes on the walls of the *ashram* at Sat Tal suggest its spirit: "Leave behind all race and class distinctions, ye that enter here," and "Here we enter into a fellowship; sometimes we will agree to differ, always we will resolve to love and unite to serve."

The members rise at five and spend an hour in devotions, sitting apart and silent on a hilltop, but joining in the *ashram* recessional hymn as they walk back in procession. Manual labor, in which all take an equal share in every kind of work, follows. Brother Stanley takes his turn as "sweeper," when staying at the *ashram*. From nine until eleven the time is occupied with lectures and discussions. Free time follows for meditation, reading, and conversation until the hour before sunset, which is spent in devotion by the lakeside, often with an address by Dr. Jones. All return together in silence to the *ashram* for the evening meal, which is vegetarian in accord with Indian custom. Silence is observed all day on Thursday until the evening service. On Sundays there is a communion service open to all Christians, followed by a period of fellowship marked by the sharing of spiritual problems.

Dr. Stanley Jones's correspondence in 1938 reveals his sense of the need for a strong central core of devoted persons at Sat Tal entirely dedicated to the *ashram* idea of sacrificial fellowship in which all privilege of status, possessions, or race is surrendered in a common life in Christ.

Since the founding of Sat Tal another *ashram* has been created by Dr. Stanley Jones in Lucknow, the capital of the United Provinces, within reach of the Lucknow Christian College. The Lucknow *ashram* carries on many activities not associated with the ancient *ashram* ideal; but it is thought of as the "expression side" of the more meditative Sat Tal. Newspaper evangelism is carried on with the Lucknow *ashram* as a base. The city has no Young Men's or Young Women's Christian Association, and the commodious building is therefore a center of Christian fellowship for young Indian men and women. Two doctors run a dispensary for the poor, and a traveling ambulance dispensary goes out to many villages. A "cold season" language school is also held for new missionaries. And a literature campaign sends out by mail tracts and gospel appeals in different languages. More closely characteristic of the traditional *ashram* principle are the visits paid by educated inquirers, Hindu, Sikh, and Moslem, who come there to study the teachings of Christ.

V

Looking round that eager circle of young Indian faces in the drawing-room of the college principal, the question inevitably arose, What are the Christian students, who have come mostly from village homes, to do with their lives? The Lindsay Commission on Christian Higher Education laid its finger on one of the weaknesses that affects the whole Christian community in India, when it criticized the lack of relationship between the Christian colleges and the Indian Christian movement as a whole. Youths think of themselves as being at college simply to become graduates, with a remunerative career to follow rather than a Christian life-vocation.

The church in India needs, for example, a church historian of genius or at any rate of authoritative scholarship and prophetic vision. There is a crying need for creative Christian architects. The new constitution calls for the growth of fundamentally Christian politicians. Asia needs an Indian Wilberforce as a Christian statesman of the outcastes and of the economically submerged; and an Indian Lincoln to lift politics above the sordidness of party recriminations and to work through administration and legislation in building a new India. The tense economic stresses and strains that tug at the Indian Christian community sound a call for skilled economists.

No bankruptcy is more tragic in Indian Christianity than the lack of a first-class intensely Indian simple literature. Indian Christendom needs not only a modern Bunyan but translators to render the Bible into language of a purity that devout Hindus will find to be truly Indian. She needs also a Punjabi Alfred Noyes, a Bengali T. S. Eliot, and a Tamil Charles Wesley to write her Christian hymns as Narayan Vaman Tilak has done for the Marathi.

She demands a Telugu Temple, and a Malayalam Fosdick, an Urdu Dean Inge, and a Hindu MacMurray to think through and restate in Asiatic categories the universal issues that must be seen afresh in their Asiatic setting; as well as an Indian Kagawa to develop the revolutionary implications of the Christian message for the social and economic structure. As we turn over the pages of such books as P. Z. Mozoomdar's *The Oriental Christ*, we long for some leader of mystical insight and intellectual clarity to be the Baron Von Hügel of Asia. We are beating the air as long as we are content to recruit and train men for the ministry without equipping them with the absolutely essential tools of first-class books. I heard a man who is a real expert say, "Christian books in India in the vernaculars are such as would not tempt one to read even on a desert island."

Professors and lecturers have a definite task in harnessing Christian technicians to the village problems of India. St. John's College, Agra, for instance, is one of the first Christian colleges in northern India to launch a sustained undertaking of research and extension work along the lines suggested by the Lindsay Commission. Its economics department has for years concentrated on a center in one of the most depressed agricultural areas in the world. They have analyzed the economic structure of the village and surveyed the method of marketing. The teachers are now more vividly and personally eager to harness their educational experience to solve problems tormenting rural

India. The students are keenly aware of the economic, chemical, and other aspects of India's agricultural life. They see their own future career in that setting. The baffling difficulties that face any attempt of this kind were revealed when the college formed a Better Farming Society in this rural district. This innocuous society was attacked by the Congress party as an attempt at European domination, by the landlord's party as a revolutionary attempt to unite tenants against their *zamindars*, and by Arya Samaj Hindu missionaries as a subtle approach to Christian proselytism.

This college has discovered a new line of work through the intensive interest of the government initiated by Lord Linlithgow's tenure of office as Viceroy. Local "village welfare" committees are being set up under the government's rural development campaign, and at the government's invitation the college is undertaking the organization, development, and guidance of these groups. When the needs of the village become central to the mind of the Christian student the future leadership of India's Christian movement will begin a new growth on sorely needed lines.

A remarkable Hindu economist, Mr. Satish Chandra Mitter, in his *A Recovery Plan for Bengal*,[1] has produced a seven-hundred-page volume that grapples in close detail with every aspect of agriculture and its multifarious crops, with irrigation, indebtedness, cooperative marketing and

[1] The Book Company Ltd., College Square, Calcutta.

banking, cottage industries, and the relation of all these both to small and to big industries, primary and technical education, transport and public health. Mr. Mitter harnesses scientific and technical skill to large-scale as well as small-scale planning; and in him it is linked with strong executive power. What he is doing points to a true path of economic salvation. As I traveled through parts of Bengal with Mr. Mitter and realized the immense good that a master spirit can achieve, especially when backed, as he is, by government good will, I felt desirous of seeing Christian leadership develop on similar lines in other and not less needy areas of India. The aim of a Christian leadership in making a recovery plan for village India will never be truly Christian unless it is directed to the helping of Hindus and Moslems as well as Christians out of the cruel privations of the present.

Indian students need, first, a quickened sense of vocation to carry the Christian vision into secular callings; and, second, dedication to the supreme tasks of the Christian pastor and teacher. An Asiatic Christian student who had visited Boston saw as he went through Copley Square the superb statue of Phillips Brooks preaching, with the figure of Christ standing behind and above him, and then in the public gardens two superbly natural and lifelike statues of other eminent pastors and preachers. He went back to his Asiatic Christian compatriots exultantly reporting that he had found, in one of the greatest spiritual and cultural centers of leadership in the Western world, the statues of pastors alongside those of presidents of the United States. India sorely needs to lift the teacher-pastor to that place of regard and honor which his calling deserves; and to harness the resources of Christian education to the creation of such a leadership as we have here surveyed.

Chapter Seven

THE BELOVED COMMUNITY

Can we now, looking back along the path that we have traveled and then trying to look forward, see the Indian Christian community both in its national and its world setting, and discover our own relation through that community to the India of tomorrow?

A universal paganism fights against the freedom of the spirit everywhere. It menaces the universal church in India, as across the world. It demands that we burn incense to the Cæsar of the nation-state or bow down to the Dagon of proletariat-man; serve the Mammon of high finance or abase ourselves at the feet of the mythical Baal of race purity. That paganism is fiercely missionary. It uses every available tool, from the moving picture to the radio and the press, for winning the devotion of youth to these idolatries. It trains its evangelists and apostles. From Tokyo to Rome the Cæsarean state, with its ritual, slogans, and shirts of many colors, organizes the life of youth. By its control of education it shapes the attitude of boys and girls and molds their standard of values.

For the ongoing Christian community this struggle for the supremacy of the spiritual and the free commerce of man's soul with his God is of supreme importance. The issue of that conflict in India depends, if the evidence that we have here surveyed is true, upon three things happening within the church. These are the development of a new Christian leadership, a cooperative facing of common tasks, and the growth of a united church in India as an integral part of the universal church.

The need for a varied and equipped leadership, lay and ministerial, Eastern and Western, unfolded itself in the last chapter and indeed throughout the book. How, we ask ourselves, can the task of calling and equipping that leadership be faced in the vast field of India and in face of the incessant and increasing flow of new life into the church, save by the pooling of our inadequate resources?

I

Contradictory feelings broke in on me as I watched the National Christian Council of India, Burma and Ceylon grappling with these questions of cooperation for the kingdom of God. That council has been created by the Protestant churches and the missionary organizations at work in those lands specifically for cooperative thinking, planning, and action.

In two years, from 1933 to 1935, the number of missionaries in India was reduced by nearly 26 per cent, from 6,030 to 4,467, a decline of 1,563. This decrease was caused by the backwash of the world depression, especially in North America, where some of the most important mission boards reduced their numbers by about one-half. The same depression simultaneously hit the Indian agriculturist, who is the backbone of self-support for the Christian church. The attempt in India to balance budgets, not only by cutting the salaries of missionaries but also by reducing the tiny salaries of village teacher-pastors below subsistence level, has driven numbers of experienced teachers reluctantly from church schools to those of the government. Thus we are faced by unheard-of increases in inquirers at the very moment when the men and the money for the work suffer catastrophic decrease. This writes across the sky in flaming letters the command to cooperate.

We see on one side the miracle of the existing Christian community in India and on the other side the task that confronts it in creating and mobilizing leaders to face the future.

The dimension and the complexity of this task is baffling, whether we think of the sheer harvesting of the multitudes pressing into the church, or of the winning of the immense populations still entrenched within Islam or Hinduism. Nor dare we omit the duty of convincing interpretation of Christ to the increasingly influential bodies of secular agnostics.

India increases her population every decade by roughly five times the present total membership of the Christian church in India, a fact which brings out one aspect of the dimensions of the work that lies ahead. Yet the growth of the Christian community in India in the last decade is unparalleled in missionary history in Asia. The present rate of increase is almost two hundred thousand a year.

So, in a meeting of the National Christian Council at Nagpur, during the last days of 1936, we tried to listen, as we looked on these fields white to harvest, for the word from God concerning these multitudes seeking to enter the church. Our bewilderment in face of them is due to the fact that God has answered the prayers of the church and that we simply did not get ready to meet the situation created by his response. What then must we now do? The disciples tugging ineffectively at the net with its multitude of fish called to their brethren in the other boat. So the harvest of the sea was landed. The call of God to the church is for instant cooperation on a scale and to a sacrificial degree never yet achieved. Denominational separatism means the door of the church slammed in the face of oncoming multitudes.

No denominational mission or church can begin to grapple alone with a problem of this size or complexity. Cooperation is not an optional addendum but the very condition of conquest. Only in comradeship can the available personnel of the church in India, whether Western or Indian, begin to reap the ripening harvest. Long-established work in sterile fields must be cut down to release men and money to deal with this urgent and glorious opportunity. To move, however, even temporarily from even unfruitful fields is terribly difficult, because at any time our prayers may be answered there, too, and we must be ready to step in when God opens the door. This is the case at the moment among the aboriginal Bhils, until recently apparently unresponsive; during 1937 twenty-seven thousand were baptized. So in those stubborn, unyielding fields we must still leave sufficient staff to be able to keep on sowing the seed until the spiritual monsoon may break and a harvest begin to sprout.

The courageous reshaping by each mission board and denominational church council of the balance of its Indian work and the re-alignment between denominations of cooperative service are nevertheless vital. Any large business that maintained its personnel in unproductive departments while customers clamored and were turned away in other departments that were understaffed would lay itself open to instant condemnation. No one who has seen the wistful waiting multitudes of India, with their faces turned toward the Light, can question where the strategy of the hour lies. Delay may bring down on our heads the condemnation that we let the precious sheaves rot in the fields rather than unite with others to garner them into the Kingdom.

The difficulties are obvious. We all have a natural reluctance—and it is strong among the rank and file of missionary subscribers in the Western churches—to leave our own project, however sterile, in order to back up a large cooperative enterprise. Yet we must brace ourselves for the sacrifice, or be in peril of setting our static wills against God's revolutionary purpose. Stagnation would deservedly come upon mission boards in the West if, in face of this cooperative work under the National Christian Council and in such a marvelous hour, they at home pursued divided counsels, followed confused and even contradictory aims, and were guilty of wasteful duplication. The inevitable consequence would be paralysis of vision, will, and action. If we accept no dictatorship from any visible or human authority, the one road toward common action lies in the steady, continuous, free planning of cooperative policies: cooperative between East and West, cooperative between denominations.

The National Christian Council also exists to tackle tasks that in the nature of things cannot be touched by any single mission board or church. Problems such as religious freedom, the distribution and sale of opium, a project for more adequate legislation on Indian Christian marriage, the disabilities of converts under marriage or other laws in Indian states, are examples of such issues of universal interest where only a national body can intervene or plan effectively.

Similarly, organizations like the Christian Literature Society for India, linked up with the National Christian Council through its Literature Committee, work cooperatively to meet the clamant need in every part of India for books, pictures, dramas, Bibles, and hymn books. In a land of many languages the best material brought into being in one language should be available through translation in all languages. National as well as regional cooperative work in this field of literature is obviously of vital importance and limitless in its horizon.

The fruits of cooperation, as the story of the National Christian Council reveals, provide a splendid harvest worth infinitely more than any sacrifice made for it. To train leaders of various communions cooperatively makes for understanding, for perspective, for happy tolerance, and for a deeper appreciation of the richness and the variety of the Christian faith and experience. The vine of cooperation bears lovely fruit: a catholic, peace-loving spirit, and personal friendships shared across denominational lines.

United training of leaders astonishingly increases educational efficiency. The best teachers are thus able to train one large group of students. The present divisive policies set overworked, undertrained men to teaching tiny groups of their own denomination numerous subjects which they cannot themselves master. Cooperation in training colleges sets at liberty funds for books, since there is but one library to support and not a dozen. Reduction of expense all round is achieved by avoiding the quadruplication of plant, running expenses, and staff. Yet these material gains, great as they are, constitute merely the by-products of the priceless spiritual gain both to the church within itself and to its appeal to the world beyond.

II

Face to face with these issues, what contribution could that little group of men and women, Indian and Western, sitting there at Nagpur, make to help forward cooperation and unity in India to meet the supreme challenge of India's seeking multitudes?

New hope springs in us when we see the National Christian Council taking fresh projects and ideas from the International Missionary Council, which embraces the whole world, and adapting them for use in India. Over thirty national and regional Christian and missionary councils, from every continent, each directly representative of churches or mission boards, have created the International Missionary Council. This council, therefore, for the first time in the four hundred years of Protestant history, creates a central Christian organism for world planning and action.

As I watched the National Christian Council at work in India, where Dr. John R. Mott, Chairman of the International Missionary Council, shared its deliberations, world cooperation to help India became a visible, practical project. In the Christian world community, there are rare prophetic spirits or organizing geniuses, writers with outstanding gifts or intellectuals capable of interpreting the gospel to critical and cultured audiences. They are all too few in number. To mobilize them for the widest use is elementary common sense and high strategy. Experiments successfully attempted in one part of the world are made available in other areas through the International Missionary Council and its national and regional groups. The brilliant achievement in Japan of newspaper evangelism is now being copied with adaptations in the Five-Year Forward Movement of Evangelism in India. Similarly, as we have mentioned, the achievement of Dr. Laubach in his splendid fight against illiteracy in the Philippine Islands is helping to gather up and focus scattered and devoted experiments already on foot not only in India but in eighteen other lands.

We have here the beginning of world planning, world sharing, and world action. The Forward Movement in Evangelism, inaugurated by the National Christian Council in 1935, is an outstanding example of nationwide cooperation, inspired by a world relationship within the International Missionary Council. This cooperative process in evangelism has, its secretary the Reverend J. Z. Hodge says, achieved at least five things. It has recalled the church in India to the central purpose of its being; quickened the Christian conscience; enlisted the lay forces of the church in active service; restored many lapsed members to the Christian fellowship; and given an impetus to closer cooperation through the realization that all Christians are "workers together with God."

Its central aim is to mobilize the Indian Christian community to carry the good news of Christ to areas still unreached. To achieve this end simple pamphlet and lyrical literature is cooperatively prepared for the stimulus and guidance of village Christian congregations and their leaders. The assistance covers hygienic and agricultural as well as moral and spiritual guidance.

The actual methods employed for the ever widening areas of witness and for conserving the results include in addition to advice from the officers of the National Christian Council: (1) small conferences to help leaders to grasp the new technical assistance rendered by, for example, Dr. Laubach's system of simplified picture teaching of adults, and to arrive at agreed standards for instruction in church worship, biblical knowledge, and church discipline both before and after baptism, as well as for the practical achievement of self-support in the Indian church; (2) visitation of areas by members of the National Christian Council's "Fellowship on Evangelism," and intervisitation between fields and denominations to share experience and encourage effort; (3) bulletins giving the story of advance achieved and a new simple literature for inquirers and converts as well as for pastors and catechists; (4) retreats and "refresher" courses to help volunteer lay leadership; and (5) the spread of simple reverent worship services especially among newly gathered village churches.

So, far from withdrawing energy from local or denominational work, this Five-Year Plan has actually quickened denominational activity all over India. The cooperative convention and the Week of Witness found throughout the whole Telugu area are but examples of numerous advances made in areas as remote as Bombay and Burma, Tinnevelly and the Punjab.

As the Indian Christian watches the seething thousands in the vast, jostling, many-colored, multiple-caste crowds at a Hindu *jathra,* or religious festival, he is tempted to feel the insignificance in numbers of his own flock. His heart is lifted out of that depression, however, as he joins the streams of Christian pilgrims who converge, for instance, upon the camping ground close to Bezwada near the east coast of Hyderabad for the three days' cooperative convention that each year draws tens of thousands of Christians for the Palm Sunday week-end.

Dusty villagers with their bundles and cooking vessels trail on foot, or travel by bus or in the train, from as far as a hundred miles away. Groups form in the shade of a tree. Students come from their colleges; clerks and merchants from towns. Hundreds of inquiring Hindus and Moslems are drawn as by a magnet to this great spiritual gathering. Indian evangelists, teachers, nurses, and doctors, with here and there missionaries of various nationalities, weave in and out of the throng of Christians of many churches—Lutheran, Baptist, Anglican, Methodist, Congregationalist, and others. You see little outward sign of organization; yet this church *jathra,* "a multitude keeping holy day," moves as one man toward the vast *pandal.* This shed, which shelters from the sun more than twelve thousand people, is set up between the flowing waters of the mighty Kistna River and a famous canal. Spiritual expectancy shines in the eyes and on the alert brown faces of those tens of thousands who, even far beyond the edge of the *pandal,* listen to the voices that through multiple loudspeakers broadcast the message.

That immense throng is held for three sessions a day, during three days in the great heat of mid-Indian April, not by moving pictures, nor by Bible dramas, but by a series of addresses by Indian, American, and British speakers, proclaiming "the unsearchable riches of Christ."

The Indian Christian who has been disheartened by the story that only outcastes become Christian, has his horizon transformed if he becomes one of the thousands of workers in the Week of Witness of, for example, the churches and the missions from America and from Europe in the Telugu country. Western Christians would be hard put to it to hide their shame at their own apathy if they saw illiterate outcaste Christian women singing hymns in village streets as part of this campaign; or groups of their children marching with banners through caste villages singing hymns, while at the end of each verse one child calls out, "To our Lord Jesus," and the rest answer in joyful chorus, "Victory."

Each year in a single week an army of voluntary Indian peasant workers by speech and song carry the message of Christ as Savior to fully eighty-five thousand villagers in over seven hundred and fifty villages. In the open street, the busy bazaar, the courtyard, or the home the story is told. Thousands of copies of Gospels and other literature are sold. Scenes strangely reminiscent of the New Testament occur. For instance, when an evangelist had been telling the story of the demoniac of Gadara, a man of unsound mind came shouting and threatening the band of preachers and teachers.

"There is a demoniac," cried someone in the crowd. "You say that the power of Christ is still the same. Can you heal him?" The evangelist took the madman by the hand and led him aside and prayed. The man was healed. The whole village was stirred. Reports after nearly a year tell us that this man has suffered no relapse.

In three clear ways these "weeks of witness" mark how the church and the missions are beginning to grapple unitedly with their task.

First, the campaigns are the direct outcome of a national will to make continuous advance, reached cooperatively by the Indian Christian leaders and by the missionaries, American, British, and European. The vision that stirred them to that decision came, as we have seen, through a world conspectus of evangelistic opportunity made by the International Missionary Council. Here then we have no sporadic effort, but a coherent plan reached deliberately in international fellowship in thought and prayer. Every report shows that leaflets produced through the National Christian Council to guide the spiritual and mental preparation of local groups of Indian Christians have been of priceless value.

Second, the movement is striking a deadly blow at the old notion which has worked as a subtle poison in the church, that evangelism is the task of the missionary while the Indian Christian community simply builds up its own inner life. It is a thrilling experience to read in translation reports written by Indian Christians in their own languages. The following sentences from a village leader could be multiplied: "We catechists and village Christians enthusiastically conducted the evangelistic campaign. With us were a group of sixteen young men who went around giving their witness by singing and acting. Their witness gave us great joy. The people gladly received the victorious gospel which we preached to them by means of pictures and singing, recitals and conversations. We preached the word of God to about one thousand eight hundred people. In the week we visited sixteen villages. The people of four villages made a request for a teacher."

This shows that Indian Christians are throwing themselves into the spread of the gospel, not wearily as a duty, but with zest and the thrill of adventure.

Third, the steadily growing proportion of caste people who listen to the Indian Christians witnessing, and who subsequently become inquirers and decide to join the church, shows how cooperative witness can stir response. Over fifty thousand caste village people have in the last decade asked for Christian instruction. Almost universally the cause is not so much ministerial preaching as lay living—the changed lives and intelligent witness of the Christian outcastes. The higher-caste people see their serfs rising to levels of life hitherto not dreamed of; and this reinforces with irresistible eloquence the Christian song and speech of these outcastes. They see that, as the National Christian Council stated in 1937, "the influences which the Spirit of Christ brings to bear upon the hearts of men inevitably tend to raise them in every respect—physical, economic, and spiritual." The church in India is seeing with increasing clearness that, as the National Christian Council adds, "to bring this gospel in its fullness to all men is simple Christian duty."

The Anglican Christians who took part in the Week of Witness in 1937 represented more than a half of the communicant membership of the church in the area concerned. The Indian bishop expressed his disappointment that not more of the membership took part. What would a Western suburban pastor say if he could get half of his flock to engage actively in practical cooperative evangelism? Large numbers of these Indian lay evangelists, too, either took the week off from their work without pay, thus losing money, or devoted to it their one short holiday period.

III

It is scarcely credible that anyone who sees realistically the task of the Christian church in India, face to face with the incoming multitude of almost two hundred thousand new members from Hinduism every year and with a nation that adds three million a year to its stupendous population, can ask whether the time has come for Western missionaries to reduce their work with a view to withdrawal. Certainly every responsible Indian Christian is eager for a strong reinforcement in India of the right kind of American, British, and European missionary. By missionaries of the right kind they mean, as Mr. E. Sambayya, a young traveling secretary of the Student Christian Movement in India, put it in a letter written after the Oxford Conference on Church, Community and State in 1937, "a new type of man and woman who is ready to learn as well as teach, receive as well as give, and be friendly as well as humble." Bishop Azariah expressed the same thought when he said to a world gathering of Christian leaders years ago, "Give us friends."

The reasons why such reinforcement from the West is essential and urgent are so numerous that we can here only catalogue the more important with bare comment.

A fundamental reason lies in the universality of the Christian church. We see in the West how tragic a calamity it is that any church should grow up with a merely national horizon. Now that for the first time in history the Christian community has roots in every nation under heaven, and when the primary curse upon man is his frantic nationalism, the Christian church in every land must be alive to its ecumenical nature. The church in India must spread its roots even more widely and deeply into its native soil, but it will fail in its mission to its own people unless it drinks in the sun and rain of God's all-bridging skies. In the West the church stands in similar need of constant openness to the message and the spirit of Asiatic and African Christian leaders. To share across the world the light that comes to men from God is the very condition of renewed vitality.

A splendid venture toward this goal is the common study during 1938 throughout India of the five universal issues that are so central to the ongoing life of the church universal that they dominate the world meeting of the International Missionary Council in December of that year at Madras. Over thirty study booklets written mainly by Indian Christian leaders with a few by Western missionaries illuminate from an Indian angle these five problems: the faith by which the church lives, the witness of the church, the life of the church, the church and its environment, and closer cooperation. The living and practical importance of these studies is illustrated by such subjects as, "The Christian attitude to the body and to suffering in the light of the doctrines of *karma*, *ahimsa*, and *maya*"[1]; "The influence of the caste system on the life of the church"; "How far can the church utilize the cultural inheritances found in India?" and "The isolation of the church from national life."

Here, then, we see in an ideal setting the true Chris-

[1] See pp. 18, 22, 97.

tian interaction of national genius and experience with the world-wide fellowship of the Christian church. The Christian church is not international in the sense of being joined together by the consenting wills of men. It is, on the contrary, one by its common life in Christ. It is one as the vine with all its branches is one, by virtue of the living sap that flows through every twig and produces flower and fruit.

The significance for India of the share that it is taking in the fellowship of thought and prayer that leads up to the Madras meeting of the International Missionary Council, and from that meeting into the future, lies in the steady development of cooperative planning and action under the guidance of the Spirit, both within India and with other Christian communities around the world.

Each people in the world has a contribution to make to all the others. Today especially, when India stands in so great need of equipped leadership, the technical skill and the gift of creative organization of colleagues from the West are essential. How many thousands of the present generation of Indian leaders are incalculably richer in their equipment through the contribution of teachers from the West who have opened up treasures of new life in India in hygiene, agriculture, medicine, music, architecture, theology, biblical interpretation, women's work, the organization of rural work, literature, psychology, broadcasting, and educational theory and practice. It is indeed interesting from a national Indian point of view to see what epoch-marking contributions have been made to the Indian Christian's understanding and use of his own Indian heritage by such American and British men as J. N. Farquhar, Hervey DeWitt Griswold, and Nicol Macnicol in literature and religious thought, H. A. Popley and R. A. Hickling in lyric and epic song. The opportunity for young missionaries to go out to India and to launch into creative work of that kind is greater and their work more urgently needed today than at any other time. Their goal should be the equipment of an ever larger and more skilled and devout company of Indian leaders.

This leads to the last of the reasons that we need to mention. To reach the untouched population of India lies far beyond the capacity of the Indian church. There are at least a hundred million more Indians today who have not heard the good news of the kingdom of God than there were when Carey landed. For the first time, however, we see an increasing tide flowing toward Christianity. To bring into India today and tomorrow some of the flower of the West will mean not only light and leading but the heartening and inspiring stimulus of helpful comradeship to the Indian leaders who now bear the brunt of this glorious yet well-nigh overwhelming task.

IV

We have now seen the essential requirement of a revolutionary development of cooperation between the Chris tian forces in India and between them and world-wide Christianity. Already we have in another chapter surveyed the third need—for a church that is Indian in its habit of thought and its pattern of life, and yet shares profound fellowship with the holy church throughout the world. That church must be at unity within itself. This principle is accepted in the process now going forward slowly toward the union of churches in South India:

> The uniting churches are agreed that in every effort to bring together divided members of Christ's body into one organization, the first aim must be the union of all who acknowledge the name of Christ in the universal church and that the test of all local schemes of union is that they should express locally the principle of the great catholic union of the body of Christ. Their desire, therefore, is so to organize the church in South India that it shall give the Indian expression of the spirit, the thought, and the life of the church universal.

Briefly the story of the movement toward unity in South India has passed through the following stages. First American, Canadian, Scottish, and English Presbyterians united in 1904 to form the Presbyterian Church in India. This not only meant union, but made for real Indian rootage. Then the churches of Congregational ancestry in the south of India united, and in 1908 the Congregational and Presbyterian groups came together in the South India United Church, to which the Malabar churches, founded by the Basel (German Swiss) Mission, joined themselves some ten years later. The present exploration in South India is to discover whether episcopal and non-episcopal churches can enter into organic unity. To go into the complex issues involved would carry us too far into the tangled brakes of ecclesiastical order and theological systems.

In North India the Presbyterians, in company with Congregationalists from western India and Welsh Calvinists from Assam, inaugurated the United Church of Northern India in 1924. Committees are now carrying on negotiations looking toward adherence to this church on the part of the Baptists, the Methodist Episcopal Church of Southern Asia, and the Congregationalists of Bengal.

Indian Christians are increasingly oppressed by the conviction that American and British Christians do not grasp the urgency of the need for union in India, nor understand the Indian attitude toward it. They say that, while Indian Christians hold strongly varying beliefs on questions of faith and order, the ecclesiastical differences have their roots mainly in the geographical accidents of occupation by the several communions of their respective areas. The scandal of bodies of Christians denying Christians of other bodies access to Holy Communion is pointed out as a grave stumbling-block to intelligent seekers.

Indian Christian thought on union moves today in the main on the following lines. Greater fellowship and closer cooperation have developed in all spheres of missionary activity in the past decade. The National Christian Council is at the center of new cooperative and coordinating efforts working for common consultation and for planning for wider united evangelism. The Council sees a new spirit of willingness to learn from the experiences of others. For this reason the project of a federation of churches is put aside as a waste of energy. It would largely duplicate the National Christian Council.

India longs to grow into one nation. The interests of the kingdom of God in India call for one visible church possessing a common life, a common ministry, and common sacraments. Only so can the church prove to the world the reality of the Christian faith. "The living present," one great Indian leader says, "oppresses the younger churches, the dead past paralyzes the older." The living present must, Indian Christians claim, triumph over the dead past. We in India, they say, face giant non-Christian forces with long history, social power, and profound philosophy. The question in India is, Shall the rule of Christ or of no-Christ prevail? "And this," says Bishop Azariah, "is of far greater moment in a land like India, China, or Japan than whether episcopacy, presbyterianism, or congregationalism shall prevail within our churches." A united front against anti-Christian forces is a matter of life or death.

Why then has not union been already achieved? The younger churches, India replies, are still largely dependent upon the older churches in the West for spiritual leadership and for financial support. Therefore a great campaign of education in the home churches has to be undertaken if union schemes in India are to come to fruition.

Bishop Azariah at the Edinburgh Conference on Faith and Order in 1937 said that the opposition to the original and daring scheme now under discussion is Indian as well as Western. We of the West are clearly called first to penitence and sorrow for our share in the divisions of Christendom; for our grievous sin in perpetuating divisions and denominational bitterness in India. There is then need for a determined will to discover a way to union; a dedication of knowledge and possessions, and a surrender of prejudices as our part of the price of union; above all a sustained agonizing share in Christ's high-priestly prayer, "That they all may be one . . . that the world may believe that thou didst send me."

We do well to contemplate in our times of quietness the great gift that that united church in India will contribute both to the West and to the Far East. Her instinct for worship and her power of sustained meditation; the beauty of her exquisite craftsmanship, which reveals her patience and persistence; her gentle grace, her loving-kindness and courtesy, are only a few of those shining qualities that should lead the Western and Far Eastern world, now preoccupied with material externals and aggressive activity, to seek after those neglected fruits of the spirit which are central in the life and teaching of our Lord.

As I wandered round the village fields that are the precincts of the unfinished Dornakal cathedral and saw an Indian peasant leading a bullock round and round grinding and mixing mortar, and women throwing broken stone through sieves in preparation for the making of cement, while other women sat cross-legged upon the ground breaking granite into cubes for the tessellated floor, and craftsmen carved the lotus, the banana bud, and the Cross in durable stone, I felt that here I had stumbled upon the true symbol of the building of the church in India.

"A church of India to justify its name," says the Bishop of Dornakal in a charge to the clergy of his diocese, a statement that may well become classical and that shall conclude our argument, "must be a branch of the universal church in this ancient land of India, in fellowship with the church throughout the world, but representing that universal church with all its catholic heritage interpreted and adapted to its national peculiarities. It will so order its life, worship, and work that the many castes and tribes of India will equally make it their spiritual home, each contributing out of its rich wealth of intellectual, social, and spiritual heritage to the consummation of the glorious ideal of the city of God."

APPENDIX

I. AREA AND POPULATION OF BRITISH INDIA AND INDIAN STATES

(Compiled from the All-India Census Report, 1931)

Provinces and States	Area in Square Miles	Population		
		Urban	Rural	Total
PROVINCES:				
Ajmer-Merwara	2,711	180,199	380,093	560,292
Andamans and Nicobars	3,143	......	29,463	29,463
Assam	55,014	213,421	8,408,830	8,622,251
Baluchistan	54,228	92,025	371,483	463,508
Bengal	77,521	3,684,330	46,429,672	50,114,002
Bihar and Orissa[1]	83,054	1,653,837	36,023,739	37,677,576
Bombay Presidency (including Aden and Sind[2])	123,679	4,953,363	16,977,238	21,930,601
Burma[3]	233,492	1,520,037	13,147,109	14,667,146
Central Provinces and Berar	99,920	1,688,470	13,819,253	15,507,723
Coorg	1,593	9,827	153,500	163,327
Delhi	573	447,442	188,804	636,246
Madras	142,277	6,337,256	40,402,851	46,740,107
Northwest Frontier Province	13,518	386,177	2,038,899	2,425,076
Punjab	99,200	3,067,464	20,513,388	23,580,852
United Provinces of Agra and Oudh	106,248	5,424,621	42,984,142	48,408,763
Total, British Territory	1,096,171	29,658,469	241,868,464	271,526,933

STATES:				
Baluchistan States	80,410	10,577	394,532	405,109
Baroda State	8,164	523,003	1,920,004	2,443,007
Bihar and Orissa States	28,648	45,715	4,606,292	4,652,007
Bombay States	27,994	607,463	3,860,933	4,468,396
Central India States	51,597	677,670	5,955,120	6,632,790
Central Provinces States	31,175	75,065	2,408,149	2,483,214
Cochin State	1,480	206,340	998,676	1,205,016
Gwalior State	26,367	395,309	3,127,761	3,523,070
Hyderabad State	82,698	1,616,981	12,819,167	14,436,148
Jammu and Kashmir State	84,516	342,314	3,303,929	3,646,243
Mysore State	29,326	1,045,042	5,512,260	6,557,302
Punjab States Agency	31,241	439,451	4,032,767	4,472,218
Rajputana States	129,059	1,556,305	9,669,407	11,225,712
Travancore State	7,625	551,788	4,544,185	5,095,973
United Provinces States	5,943	126,138	1,079,932	1,206,070
Western India States Agency	35,442	883,776	3,115,474	3,999,250
Other States and Agencies	50,823	224,021	4,212,046	4,436,067
Total, Indian States	712,508	9,326,958	71,983,887	81,310,845
Grand Total, India	1,808,679	38,985,427	313,852,351	352,837,778

[1] Orissa was constituted a separate province with Cuttack as capital on April 1, 1936.

[2] On April 1, 1936, Sind was constituted a separate province with Karachi as its capital. Aden was made a crown colony on April 1, 1937.

[3] On April 1, 1937, Burma was separated from India.

II. LITERACY[1]

Religion	Numbers per thousand who are literate for all ages, five and over								
	1931			1921			1911		
	PERSONS	MALES	FEMALES	PERSONS	MALES	FEMALES	PERSONS	MALES	FEMALES
All Religions	95	156	29	82	139	21	69	122	12
Hindu	84	144	21	75	130	16	64	116	9
Sikh	91	138	29	68	107	16	77	121	16
Moslem	64	107	15	53	93	9	44	80	5
Christian	279	352	203	285	355	210	253	339	159

[1] Reprinted from *The Statesman's Year-Book*, 1935, p. 126. London, Macmillan and Co., 1935.

III. POPULATION BY RELIGION[1]

INDIA AND BURMA

	1921 Census	*1931 Census*	*Increase or Decrease*
Hindu (Total)	216,734,586	239,195,140	+10.4
Moslem	68,735,233	77,677,545	+13
Buddhist	11,571,268	12,786,806	+10.5
Sikh	3,238,803	4,335,771	+33.9
Primitive Religions	9,774,611	8,280,347	−15.3
Christian	4,754,064	6,296,763	+32.5
Jain	1,178,596	1,252,105	+ 6.2
Zoroastrian	101,778	109,752	+ 7.8
Jews	21,778	24,141	+10.9
Unreturned	......	2,879,438	....
Total	316,128,721	352,837,778	+10.6

[1] Reprinted from *Directory of Christian Missions and Churches in India, Burma and Ceylon*, 1936–1937, p. 36.

IV. DISTRIBUTION OF HINDU COMMUNITY[1]

Brahmans	15,237,452
Caste Hindus	171,190,624
Non-caste Hindus (Depressed Classes)	52,194,526
Undetermined	572,538
Total	239,195,140

[1] Reprinted from *Directory of Christian Missions and Churches in India, Burma and Ceylon*, 1936–1937, p. 39.

V. CHRISTIAN EDUCATION IN INDIA[1]

	Institutions	*Students*
Elementary Schools	13,274	609,821
Secondary Schools	302	67,229
Colleges	31	11,163
Theological Schools	25	556
Bible Training Schools	74	2,855
Teacher Training Schools	63	3,153

[1] Figures furnished by the International Missionary Council on the basis of reports of 1935–1936.

VI. CHRISTIANS IN INDIA AND BURMA[1]

ALL RACES AND SECTS

(Indian and European)

1891	2,284,380	1921	4,754,664
1901	2,923,241	1931	6,296,763
1911	3,876,203	1936	7,304,255 (estimate)

BY RACE

	1921	*1931*
European and allied races	175,737	167,771
Anglo-Indians	113,041	138,758
Indians	4,464,396	5,990,234
Total	4,753,174	6,296,763

BY SECTS, ALL RACES

	1921	*1931*	*Increase per cent*
Protestants	2,136,835	3,002,558	+41
Roman Catholics	1,823,079	2,113,659	+16
Romo-Syrians	423,968	654,939	+55
Syrians	367,588	525,607	+43
Armenians and Greeks	1,704	......	....
Total	4,753,174	6,296,763	+32.5

TOTAL CHRISTIANS IN URBAN AND RURAL AREAS

	Towns	*Population*	*Christians*
Provinces	1,695	29,531,256	950,670
States	877	9,326,958	323,547
Total Urban Areas	2,572	38,858,214	1,274,217
Compared with Rural Areas		313,979,564	5,022,546

[1] All tables on this page are reprinted from *Directory of Christian Missions and Churches in India, Burma and Ceylon*, 1936–1937, pp. 38 and 39.

READING LIST

This list is selected from the very wide range of literature on India and is in no sense exhaustive. The views of the authors represented here are not necessarily in harmony with those of author of this book. Several older books have been included because of their special value as reference sources, and even though out of print will be found in most libraries. Leaders of study groups using this book will find most helpful "A Course for Adults on India," by T. H. P. Sailer, available from denominational literature headquarters for twenty-five cents.

General and Descriptive

India Reveals Herself. Basil Mathews and Winifred Wilson. New York, Oxford University Press, 1937. $2.50.

Indian Commentary, An. Rev. ed. G. T. Garratt. New York, Jonathan Cape and Harrison Smith, 1930. $2.75.

Land and Life of India, The. Margaret Read. London, Edinburgh House Press, 1934. (Available from Missionary Education Movement, 80 cents.)

Living India. Lady Mabel H. Hartog. London, Blackie and Son, Ltd., 1936. 2/6.

Renascent India: from Ram Mohan Roy to Mohandas Gandhi. H. C. H. Zacharias. New York, E. P. Dutton & Co., 1933. $3.25.

Statistical Abstract for British India, . . . from 1924-25 to 1933-34. Delhi, Manager of Publications, 1936.

Voiceless India. Gertrude Emerson. Garden City, N. Y., Doubleday, Doran & Co., 1930. (Out of print.)

History and Politics

Cambridge Shorter History of India. New York, The Macmillan Co., 1934. 3 parts in 1 volume. $4.00.

Case for India, The. John S. Hoyland. New York, E. P. Dutton & Co., 1929. $2.00.

Dyarchy in Practice. A. Appadorai. New York, Longmans, Green & Co., 1937. $3.50.

Reading List

INDIA AND BRITAIN. C. F. Andrews. London, Student Christian Movement Press, 1937. Cheaper ed. 2/6.

INDIAN ADMINISTRATION. G. N. Joshi. New York, The Macmillan Co., 1937. $2.25.

INDIAN GODS AND KINGS: THE STORY OF A LIVING PAST. E. Hawkridge. Boston, Houghton Mifflin Co., 1935. $3.50.

INDIA'S NEW CONSTITUTION. J. P. Eddy and F. H. Lawton. New York, The Macmillan Co., 1935. $2.10.

LEGACY OF INDIA, THE. G. T. Garratt, editor. New York, Oxford University Press, 1937. $4.00.

NATIONHOOD FOR INDIA. J. S. M. Meston. New Haven, Yale University Press, 1933. $1.50.

OXFORD STUDENT'S HISTORY OF INDIA. 13th ed. Vincent A. Smith. New York, Oxford University Press, 1931. $1.35.

POLITICAL INDIA, 1832-1932: A CO-OPERATIVE SURVEY OF A CENTURY. Sir John G. Cumming, ed. New York, Oxford University Press, 1932. $1.50.

SKETCH OF THE HISTORY OF INDIA FROM 1858 TO 1918. H. H. Dodwell. New York, Longmans, Green & Co., 1925. $2.25.

Rural Conditions and Movements

BEHIND MUD WALLS. William H. and Charlotte V. Wiser. New York, Richard R. Smith, 1930. $1.50. (Available from Harper & Brothers.)

HINDU JAJMANI SYSTEM, THE. William H. Wiser. Lucknow, Lucknow Publishing House, 1936. Rs. 2-8-0.

INDIAN PEASANT, THE. Marquis of Linlithgow. London, Faber & Faber, 1932. Paper, 1/–.

INDIAN PEASANT UPROOTED, THE. Margaret Read. New York, Longmans, Green & Co., 1931. $2.50.

RURAL WELFARE IN INDIA, 1936. C. F. Strickland. New York, Oxford University Press, 1936. 25 cents.

SEEN AND HEARD IN A PUNJAB VILLAGE. Miriam Young. London, Student Christian Movement Press, 1931. 5/–.

UP FROM POVERTY IN RURAL INDIA. D. Spencer Hatch. 3rd ed. New York, Oxford University Press, 1936. $1.50.

Social and Economic Problems

CASTE AND RACE IN INDIA. G. S. Ghurye. New York, Alfred A. Knopf, 1932. $4.00.

Reading List

CHAMARS, THE. G. W. Briggs. Religious Life of India Series. New York, Oxford University Press, 1920. $2.00.

FREEDOM. Welthy Honsinger Fisher. New York, Friendship Press, 1930. Cloth, 75 cents; paper, 25 cents.

INDIA'S SOCIAL HERITAGE. L. S. S. O'Malley. New York, Oxford University Press, 1934. $2.00.

KEY OF PROGRESS, THE: A SURVEY OF THE STATUS AND CONDITIONS OF WOMEN IN INDIA. A. R. Caton, ed. New York, Oxford University Press, 1930. $2.50.

MODERN INDIA: A CO-OPERATIVE SURVEY. Rev. ed. Sir John G. Cumming, ed. New York, Oxford University Press, 1932. $1.50.

OUR CAUSE: A SYMPOSIUM BY INDIAN WOMEN. Shyam Kumari Nehru, ed. Allahabad, Kitabistan Press, 1937. Rs. 7-3-9.

POVERTY AND POPULATION IN INDIA. Dattatraya G. Karve. New York, Oxford University Press, 1936. $1.50.

WITHOUT THE PALE: THE LIFE STORY OF AN OUTCASTE. M. S. Stevenson. New York, Oxford University Press, 1931. $1.25.

Indian Religions and Philosophy

BHAGAVAD GITA, THE. Translated by A. W. Ryder. Chicago, University of Chicago Press, 1929. $2.00.

CONTEMPORARY THOUGHT OF INDIA. Alfred C. Underwood. New York, Alfred A. Knopf, 1931. (Out of print.)

CROWN OF HINDUISM, THE. J. N. Farquhar. New York, Oxford University Press, 1917. $2.00.

HINDU VIEW OF LIFE, THE. S. Radhakrishnan. New York, The Macmillan Co., 1927. $2.00.

INDIA AND ITS FAITHS: A TRAVELER'S RECORD. J. B. Pratt. Boston, Houghton Mifflin Co., 1915. $4.00.

INDIAN ISLAM. Murray T. Titus. Religious Quest of India Series. New York, Oxford University Press, 1930. $4.50.

INDIAN THOUGHT AND ITS DEVELOPMENT. Albert Schweitzer. New York, Henry Holt & Co., 1936. $2.50.

INSIGHTS INTO MODERN HINDUISM. Hervey deW. Griswold. New York, Henry Holt & Co., 1934. $2.00.

LIVING RELIGIONS OF THE INDIAN PEOPLE, THE. Nicol Macnicol. London, Student Christian Movement Press, 1934. (Available from Missionary Education Movement, New York, $3.50.)

MODERN RELIGIOUS MOVEMENTS IN INDIA. J. N. Farquhar. New York, The Macmillan Co., 1924. (Out of print.)

Reading List

Education

Christian College in India, The: report of the commission on christian higher education in india. New York, Oxford University Press, 1931. $2.00.

Christian Education in India. Sir George Anderson and Bishop Henry Whitehead. New York, The Macmillan Co., 1932. $1.50.

Christian Education in the Villages of India. Alice B. Van Doren. New York, International Missionary Council, 1931. 80 cents.

Christian High Schools in India. Alice B. Van Doren. London, Student Christian Movement Press, 1937. 4/6.

Education of India: a study of british educational policy in india, 1835-1920. A Mayhew. London, Faber & Gwyer, 1926. 10/6.

Indian Nationalism and the Christian Colleges. P. J. Braisted. New York, Association Press, 1935. $2.00.

New Schools for Young India. William J. McKee. Chapel Hill, University of North Carolina Press, 1930. $4.50.

Christianity in India

All in the Day's Work. Godfrey E. Phillips. New York, Missionary Education Movement, 1929. Boards, 50 cents; paper, 25 cents.

Builders of the Indian Church. Stephen Neill. London, Edinburgh House Press, 1934. (Available from Missionary Education Movement, New York, 80 cents.)

Cameos from Purulia. L. Margaret Sharpe. New York, American Mission to Lepers, 1936. 35 cents.

Christ of the Indian Road. E. Stanley Jones. New York, Abingdon Press, 1925. $1.00.

Christ's Way to India's Heart. J. Waskom Pickett. Lucknow, Lucknow Publishing House, 1937. (Available from Missionary Education Movement, New York, 50 cents.)

Christian Mass Movements in India. J. Waskom Pickett. New York, Abingdon Press, 1933. (Available from International Missionary Council, New York, $1.00.)

Christian Mission in Rural India, The. Kenyon L. Butterfield. New York, International Missionary Council, 1930. Paper, 80 cents.

Reading List

CHRISTIAN UNION IN SOUTH INDIA: AN ADVENTURE IN FELLOWSHIP. W. J. Noble. London, Student Christian Movement Press, 1936. 2/–.

CHRISTIANITY IN THE EASTERN CONFLICTS. William Paton. New York, Friendship Press, 1937. Cloth, $1.50; paper, 75 cents. (Especially Chapter III.)

DINABANDHU: A BACKGROUND BOOK ON INDIA. Ruth Isabel Seabury. New York, Friendship Press, 1938. Cloth, $1.00; paper, 60 cents.

DIRECTORY OF CHRISTIAN MISSIONS AND CHURCHES IN INDIA, BURMA AND CEYLON, 1936-1937. Nagpur, National Christian Council, 1936. Rs. 2-8.

FRONTIER PEOPLES OF INDIA, THE: A MISSIONARY SURVEY. Alexander McLeish. New York, World Dominion Press, 1931. $1.50.

HERITAGE OF BEAUTY: PICTORIAL STUDIES OF MODERN CHURCH ARCHITECTURE IN ASIA AND AFRICA, ILLUSTRATING THE INFLUENCE OF INDIGENOUS CULTURES. Daniel J. Fleming. New York, Friendship Press, 1937. $1.50.

INDIA AND THE CHRISTIAN MOVEMENT. V. S. Azariah. New York, National Council of the Protestant Episcopal Church, 1938. Paper, 25 cents.

INDIA LOOKS TO HER FUTURE. Oscar M. Buck. New York, Friendship Press, 1930. Cloth, 50 cents; paper, 25 cents.

INDIAN APPROACH TO INDIA, AN. Milton Stauffer, editor. New York, Missionary Education Movement, 1927. Cloth, 50 cents; paper, 25 cents.

MOVING MILLIONS: THE PAGEANT OF MODERN INDIA. A Symposium. Boston, Central Committee on the United Study of Foreign Missions and Missionary Education Movement, 1938. Cloth, $1.00; paper, 50 cents.

RATS, PLAGUE, AND RELIGION. John S. Carman. Philadelphia, American Baptist Publication Society, 1936. $1.25.

UNTOUCHABLES' QUEST, THE. Godfrey Phillips. New York, Friendship Press, 1936. Cloth, 75 cents; paper, 40 cents.

Biography

ALEXANDER DUFF, PIONEER OF MISSIONARY EDUCATION. William Paton. New York, George H. Doran Co., 1923. (Out of print.)

AMERICAN DOCTOR AT WORK IN INDIA, AN. Sir William Wanless. New York, Fleming H. Revell Co., 1932. $1.50.

Reading List

AUTOBIOGRAPHY: WITH MUSINGS ON RECENT EVENTS IN INDIA. Jawaharlal Nehru. London, John Lane, 1936. 15/–.

CHILDREN OF THE LIGHT IN INDIA: BIOGRAPHIES OF NOTED INDIAN CHRISTIANS. Rebecca J. Parker. New York, Fleming H. Revell Co., 1930. (Out of print.)

MAHATMA GANDHI: HIS OWN STORY. C. F. Andrews, editor. New York, The Macmillan Co., 1930. (Out of print.)

MAHATMA GANDHI AT WORK: HIS OWN STORY CONTINUED. C. F. Andrews, editor. New York, The Macmillan Co., 1931. $2.50.

NARAYAN VAMAN TILAK, THE CHRISTIAN POET OF MAHARASHTRA. J. C. Winslow. Builders of Modern India Series. New York, Association Press, 1923. $1.50.

PANDITA RAMABAI SARASVATI, PIONEER IN THE MOVEMENT FOR THE EDUCATION OF THE CHILD-WIDOW OF INDIA. Clementina Butler. New York, Fleming H. Revell Co., 1922. (Out of print.)

SADHU SUNDAR SINGH. C. F. Andrews. New York, Harper & Brothers, 1934. $1.00.

SUSIE SORABJI, CHRISTIAN-PARSEE EDUCATIONALIST OF WESTERN INDIA. Cornelia Sorabji. New York, Oxford University Press, 1932. $1.50.

WILLIAM CAREY. S. Pearce Carey. New York, George H. Doran Co., 1923. (Out of print.)

INDEX

Index

Index

Index

Index